THE NO-PAIN RESUME WORKBOOK

A Complete Guide to Job-Winning Resumes

THE NO-PAIN RESUME WORKBOOK
A Complete Guide to Job-Winning Resumes

Hiyaguha Cohen

BUSINESS ONE IRWIN
Homewood, Illinois 60430

Sponsoring editor: Jeffrey A. Krames
Project editor: Karen Murphy
Production manager: Carma W. Fazio
Jacket Designer: Renee Klyczek Nordstrom
Compositor: Eastern Graphics Typographers
Typeface: 11/13 Century Schoolbook
Printer: Edwards Brothers, Inc.

Library of Congress Cataloging-in-Publication Data

Cohen, Hiyaguha.
    The no-pain resume workbook : a complete guide to job-winning
resumes / Hiyaguha Cohen.
        p.   cm.
    ISBN 1-55623-577-1
    1. Rèsumès (Employment)   I. Title.
HF5383.C627   1992
650.14—dc20   91–25425

Printed in the United States of America

1 2 3 4 5 6 7 8 9 0 EB 8 7 6 5 4 3 2 1 0

ACKNOWLEDGMENTS

"Daring enthusiasm and abiding cheerfulness
Can accomplish everything on earth
Without fail."

—Sri Chimmoy

With my heart's gratitude to Sri Chinmoy, for helping me to see the humor and light in everything—even in resumes.

And to my saintly spouse Sudheya, who read every page, offered brilliant suggestions, cheered ceaselessly, and even cooked and cleaned while I pursued "my art." I certainly couldn't have written this book without his support and help.

Finally, thanks to all the many people who enthusiastically participated in this book's birth. Especially, Vanda Sendzimer, Scott Badler, Khipra, Renuka, Laurie Midlin, Judith Rosenberg, Wickie Stamps, Lynn Liccardo, and my wonderful Dad, David Cohen.

Hiyaguha Cohen

INTRODUCTION

"Your resume is more than just a piece of paper: it is a piece of paper with lies written all over it. Often, a good resume can mean the difference between not getting a job and not even coming close."

—Dave Barry, *Claw Your Way to the Top*

Three major shocks usher us out of childhood. First, we learn that there really is no Santa Claus. Then, we discover that people die and don't come back. Finally, we realize that we've been tossed from the parental nest—we must write a resume and get a job.

After each of these events, we look down the black tunnel of despair and wish it wasn't so. But life forces us forward in spite of our protests, and eventually we must engage in the world of mature things.

And so, dear reader, you are about to write your resume. Gone are the carefree days when nobody asked about your credentials—the time has come to document yourself. True, a trip to the Caribbean would be much more fun, but you need a job to pay for a trip to the Caribbean, and you need a resume to get a job.

So plunge ahead! It won't be that bad. This book will hold your hand and lead you step-by-step through the resume writing process. It may even provoke a chuckle along the way. Writing your resume will be fun and easy!

HOW TO USE THIS BOOK

The No-Pain Resume Workbook doesn't waste space preaching resume philosophy. It won't make you rifle through scores of sample resumes looking for a good one to copy. You won't need to obsess about wording or format. Just fill in the blanks, and you'll end up with a unique and powerful resume—in fact, the best resume ever.

Each chapter in the *Workbook* will take you through a new section of the resume, providing useful information, a few good jokes, and a worksheet. The worksheets provide sample wording that you can use—all you do is fill in the blanks. If you want to modify the wording provided, you can refer to the sample resumes in Appendix 2 for inspiration.

When you complete each worksheet, you'll transfer your responses to a Resume Format Sheet. (The Format Sheets look like the forms you fill out when you file your taxes, but they're more benign.) Appendix 1 contains nine different Format Sheets. Each Format Sheet provides a complete template for a particular type of resume. For instance, you'll find formats for a Student Resume, for a Technical Resume, and for a Consultant's Resume. Just pick the Format Sheet that suits your particular professional needs and enter the information from your worksheet. When you finish transferring information from all of your worksheets, you'll have a complete resume, ready for typing. It couldn't be easier!

TABLE OF CONTENTS

CHAPTER 1

RESUME ABCs

"I'm sorry, son. I've reviewed your resume, and you lack the necessary credentials to qualify for presents."

WHAT'S THE REAL PURPOSE OF A RESUME?

Bet you thought the real purpose of a resume was to get a job, didn't you? Guess what? The real purpose of a resume *is* to get a job. (Of course, thick beige resumes also make lovely placemats.)

Okay, let's get serious. Many people think that resumes should accurately portray what they've done in the past, so they dutifully list all of their jobs in chronological order. Their resumes are boring, hard to read, and ineffective.

Since you aren't a boring person, your resume shouldn't be a bore. Your resume should entice readers. How can you entice readers if your work history is disastrous and you dropped out of school? Don't worry— good resumes do more than merely list job duties: they also tell readers what you're *capable* of doing. They highlight your strengths, obscure your problems, and let employers know, right up at the top, that you have the very skills they so desperately need.

Your resume is not an epitaph. It needs to live and breathe. Good resumes speak to employers, charm them into interviewing you, and guide the conversation during interviews. "Oh, I see you enjoy clam-digging," the interviewer comments, scanning your resume for interesting tidbits. "Indeed, I do. I'm champion clam-digger of the Northeast," you answer, profoundly impressing the interviewer.

When you leave the interviewer's office, your resume stays behind. The interviewer may forget your face, but your resume reminds him that you're the nice clam-digger who excels at everything. After a while, when he has a pile of resumes and can't remember any matching faces, your resume convinces him that you're the best. So you see, your resume pitches your case before *and* after the interview. Remember this as you design your resume, always asking yourself, "What would make someone want to meet me, and what might help them remember me?"

RESUME FLAVOR

Most resumes fall into one of three categories: the *chronological, functional,* or *combination* format.

The most conservative, boring resumes list jobs and schooling in reverse *chronological* order, without much other information. Although personnel officers often recommend this format, research shows that juicier resumes yield better results.

Many experts tout the advantages of the *functional* format, which lists skills and accomplishments at the top of the resume. The Work History section appears at the bottom (or not at all), and lists only your job titles and the names of the companies you worked for, without any descriptive text telling exactly what you did in each job.

Functional resumes work well for job hoppers, career changers, graduates with no real work experience, and others who have something to hide. They let you showcase the skills you gained pursuing hobbies or volunteer work, and downplay the sorry truth about your work life.

In spite of their advantages, functional resumes present a big problem: employers suspect that you have something to hide the minute they see the functional format. If you must use a functional resume, you need to be very artful. See Chapter 15, "Special Problems," for guidance.

For average job seekers, the *combination* resume offers the best option. This format presents skills and accomplishments at the top of the resume, but also provides a detailed description of the job duties performed in each position.

This book focuses on combination resumes, but also provides guidelines for those with special needs.

EIGHT RESUME COMMANDMENTS

1. Humility Doesn't Rhyme with Resume
"Modesty—the art of drawing attention to whatever it is you're being humble about."

—Bits and Pieces

"'Love Soap' does a pretty good job"—What a stupid advertisement that would be. Your resume is your personal advertisement. If you don't toot your own horn, your resume will be as stupid as that 'Love Soap' ad.

Bad manners, you think, to boast and make a big deal out of your petty accomplishments? Your resume isn't an application to Miss Snod's Charm School. So adjust your humble attitude right now and prepare to brag.

By the way, in case you happen to be naturally bombastic, you do need to exercise some restraint. You can't come right out and state, "I'm brilliant, talented, and available: hire me." The artful resume wears a modest veneer; it may shamelessly wave your flag, but it does so in a most dignified way.

2. Statistics Give Employers Great Joy

"Grown-ups love figures . . . If you were to say to the grown-ups: 'I saw a beautiful house made of rosy brick, with geraniums in the windows and doves on the roof,' they would not be able to get any idea of that house at all. You would have to say to them: 'I saw a house that cost $20,000.' Then they would exclaim: 'Oh, what a pretty house that is!'"

—Saint-Exupery, *The Little Prince*

All employers speak "statistics." When your boss is unhappy with your performance, she won't say, "I'm disappointed in you." She'll say, "Your efficiency has dropped 30 percent in the past three months," or, "Your predecessor did $120,000 worth of business and you only did half of that."

To communicate with employer types, you need to speak their language. You will never impress employers by claiming, "I made lots of profits for my last boss." Instead, you must announce that you were ranked Number One in your district and that you raked in $600K; employers will swoon. Not only because your statistics reveal your greatness, but also because employers relax when they see numbers. If you have good numbers, you can't be a thief, pervert, incompetent, or lazy slob, can you?

So get your numbers down on paper. Promoted three times in seven years? Managed a $70,000 budget? Recruited seven new customers? Quantify your accomplishments, then write them down.

3. Scour Your Memory

Great chefs put all the ingredients on the table before starting to cook. They don't rip around the kitchen in the middle of making a delicate sauce screaming, "Where's the thyme, the mustard, the flour?"

Before you start writing, probe your memory. Did you have a two-month research job in 1973 that you forgot about? Did you win awards in college? Did you get promoted in your first job? List all your accomplishments on paper, starting with your most recent ones and stretching back as far as you can remember. Each time you write down an achievement, it's like a deposit in the bank. All your achievements, no matter how little, enhance your wealth. When you write your resume, you can withdraw whatever you need from your achievement bank.

If you have trouble remembering all the great things you've done, don't worry: the worksheets at the end of each chapter will help to jog your memory.

4. Short Is Beautiful

An extra-long resume doesn't impress employers—more likely, it will bore them to death. Your resume should be one page if you haven't been working long, or two pages if you have considerable work experience.

You've heard that a resume should never exceed one page? In fact, research shows that employers don't mind two-page resumes if you have considerable experience. Just make sure that the first page convinces employers to turn to the second. If you want to list all your outstanding qualifications on the first page, use a Spotlight section at the top (see Chapter 4).

5. Don't Copycat Another Resume

Most resume guidebooks provide a few pages of text and 100 pages of sample resumes. People just like you buy those books and then copycat resumes from them, merely substituting their own names and job titles. Can you imagine?

What? You thought about doing it yourself? Don't be foolish. To copy another person's resume is as silly as copying another person's income tax form. Your goals, background, and personality are unique, and you deserve a unique resume.

Use the sample resumes at the back of this book for inspiration, but don't plagiarize. This book makes it easy for you to write your very own resume without resorting to treachery or deceit.

6. Speak the Right Language

If you want to get a job, never, EVER use the word "I" in your resume.

You ask, "Why can't I use the 'I' word when my resume is all about *me*?" Well, it's one of those fake humble things we mentioned before.

Employers think the "I" pronoun shows egotism. If you say, "I mopped floors," you could be implying that you think you're really special— "*I, I, I* (nobody else) mopped the floors, ha ha." But "mopped floors" sounds really self-effacing.

To get around the pronoun problem, start all sentences describing yourself with verbs. Instead of saying, "I cooked grits," say "Cooked grits."

Why verbs? Verbs, like statistics, thrill employers. Employers think that the more verbs you use, the more dynamic you are. You've got to admit, "Purchased room deodorizer" sounds more energetic than "Responsible for purchasing room deodorizer."

You disagree? You think that "*responsible for*" sounds more businesslike and dignified? So do lots of other job seekers whose resumes end up in the rejection pile. Employers don't care how dignified you are. They know that many dignified workers snooze at their desks all day long. Verbs show employers that you're the energetic, dynamic type of worker who will get the job done.

7. Accuracy Matters

"I see here that you worked for Hypertech, Inc. from 1883 to 1990."

A typo or misspelled word in your resume tells employers that you're lazy or sloppy or stupid; none of these attributes will get you hired. Check and recheck your resume. Have a friend proofread it just to be sure. And make absolutely certain that your address and telephone number are correct and current.

8. Resumes Are Sober Things

Do not have graphics, touches of humor, or anything overly creative in your resume. A resume is a sober thing.

On the other hand, every rule permits exceptions. Certain professions, such as advertising and graphic arts, allow creative resumes. And, there are rare souls in all professions who appreciate the exotic. If you *must* use humor in your resume or run it off on purple paper or insert graphics, go ahead. You just *may* get the interview you want, if you want something offbeat.

PART 1

STEP-BY-STEP THROUGH
THE RESUME

Instructions: In the next section, you will compose your resume. Follow these steps (put a check mark next to each step after you complete it):

☐ 1. Go to Appendix 1 at the end of this book. There, you find nine different types of Resume Format Sheets. Each provides a template for a particular type of resume. Decide which Resume Format Sheet you want to use:

- *Professional Resume with Summary Statement*, page A-2
- *Professional Resume with Highlights*, page A-5
- *Professional Resume with Skills Section*, page A-8
- *Consultant/Freelancer Resume*, page A-14
- *Technical Resume*, page A-11
- *Student/Recent Graduate Resume*, page A-18
- *Artist/Writer/Performer Resume*, page A-20
- *Too Many Years in Same Job Resume* (also useful if you've had only one job in your chosen field), page A-23
- *Career Changer/Special Problems Resume*, page A-26

Note: If you have difficulty choosing among the three types of professional resumes, wait until you finish reading Chapter 4, "Getting in the Spotlight," before making your final choice.

☐ 2. Carefully remove the Resume Format Sheet that you want to use, tearing along the perforated edge.

☐ 3. Keep your Resume Format Sheet close by. Turn the page and read the next chapter.

☐ 4. Complete the worksheet at the end of the chapter.

☐ 5. Transfer the information from the worksheet to your Resume Format Sheet. If your Resume Format Sheet doesn't provide enough room to enter your information, attach additional sheets as needed.

☐ 6. Stare out the window and collect your thoughts. If you don't have a window or a thought, make a solemn vow to get one soon.

☐ 7. Repeat steps 3 through 6 for all the chapters in this section. Feel free to make a cup of tea at any time.

☐ 8. Done? You now have a complete, formatted resume, ready for typing.

Important Notes: Make sure that you remove the heading from your Format Sheet before typing your resume. The first line of your resume should contain only your name.

Also: Even though most of the Format Sheets exceed two pages in length, your final typed resume should NOT be longer than two pages. The headers and instructions lengthen the Format Sheets.

Finally: If none of the Resume Format Sheets meet your needs, don't worry. Simply complete the worksheet at the end of each chapter. Then transfer the information to a blank sheet of paper, following the format of any sample resume that you like from Appendix 2.

CHAPTER 2

THE RESUME HEADING

"Fools' names, like fools' faces, are often seen in public places."

—Thomas Fuller

In the Heading section of the resume, you can really shine. Even if you have no work experience and no education at all, you have a name, and this is where to flaunt it.

The heading consists of your name, address, and telephone number. Sound ridiculously straightforward? Don't be fooled. Even the Heading section of your resume must be crafted with savvy and care.

MAKE YOUR NAME HAUNT THE READER

Think about the impact that names have. If a resume says "Pope John Paul" right at the top, you don't care about the rest of the credentials. The name says it all.

What does this have to do with humble you? You can't write "Pope John Paul" on top of *your* resume. True, but if you use a few special tricks, you *can* give your name extra impact. Not by donning a pseudonym, not by adding British touches (*Lady* Jane Smith *III*), but by employing simple formatting techniques.

First, make your name stand out so it leaves an indelible impression. Capitalize all the letters, and use boldface type if you have it. Try skipping a line between your name and address so that your name sits on a line by itself. And be sure to put your name in the upper left corner of the second page, again capitalized and bold.

Should you use your middle name? It doesn't matter; if you like it, use it. Any special advice for exotic names, like "Rashid" or "Hiyaguha"? By all means, proudly exhibit your unique moniker; readers definitely take note of unusual names and remember them more readily than mundane ones.

Why all this concern about making readers notice your name? Because a boldly stated name, like a firm handshake, conveys the subliminal message that you're a confident professional. Plus, when readers remember your name, they unconsciously feel that they've met you before.

THE REST OF THE HEADING

After your name, tell readers where to find you. Center your address under your name, in regular type, and center your phone number under your address. It looks classier to write out words instead of abbreviating, so avoid shortcuts in your address if possible (121 Farmer Street, Berkeley, California; *not* 121 Farmer St., Berkeley, CA).

Don't capitalize or boldface the address or phone number—you'll draw attention away from your name. Check, double-check, and triple-check for accuracy. A great resume with a wrong phone number equals tragedy.

Should you list your work number on your resume? Probably not. You don't want to give prospective employers the impression that you use work time for personal matters, do you?

What about including a second address or phone number, if you have two residences? Don't do it: employers will think that you're too flighty or too wealthy. List just one number, and if possible, have an answering machine pick up your calls when you can't.

You can either center your heading or left align it, leaving a half-inch to one-inch margin on top. In either case, adding a line or double line under the heading sets it off nicely. See the examples below:

CENTERED HEADING

```
                    JOHN SMITH

                 18 Weatherby Road
                Aspen, Colorado  21121
                   (303) 273-4312




OBJECTIVE:

A fun job with no pressure and a high salary.
```

LEFT-ALIGNED HEADING

```
JOHN SMITH
18 Weatherby Road
Aspen, Colorado  21121                      (303) 273-4312




OBJECTIVE:

A fun job with no pressure and a high salary.
```

WORKSHEET

Heading

Instructions: Review the checklist below. Then turn to Appendix 2 and examine the headings on the sample resumes. Go to your Resume Format Sheet and fill in your heading information. If you don't like the heading style your format sheet uses, indicate the changes you want in the left margin.

HEADING DOs

- ☐ Capitalize all the letters in your name.
- ☐ Use bold type for your name.
- ☐ Leave a margin of one-half inch to one inch above the heading.
- ☐ Skip at least three lines below the heading.
- ☐ Add a line or double line below the heading if it is left-aligned (optional for centered headings).
- ☐ Check and double-check to make sure that your address and phone number are correct.

SECOND PAGES

- ☐ List your name and the page number in a header.

JOHN SMITH
Page 2

AWARDS:
- First prize, Aurora jugglers
- Finalist, Betty Crocker
  Bake-Off

REFERENCES:
Available on request.

CHAPTER 3

THE JOB OBJECTIVE

TRASH YOUR JOB OBJECTIVE RIGHT NOW

"Every man is, or hopes to be, an Idler."

—Samuel Johnson

Here's a fun thing to do. Ask a group of kids what they want to be when they grow up. You'll get responses like this: "I want to be a circus clown." "I want to be an astronaut." "I want to eat chocolate ice cream all day and night and never go to bed." Kids give honest answers.

Now ask a group of adults what they would do if they won the lottery. "I'd retire to the Caribbean and snorkel all day." "I'd buy a ranch in Montana." "I'd finally write my novel." "I'd eat chocolate ice cream all day and night and never go to bed."

NOW, take a stack of resumes and read the job objectives. "A challenging position in advanced biotechnical research at a large university." "An entry level administrative position utilizing my excellent typing and organizational skills."

Employers must be dummies if they believe that stuff. Even so, they certainly don't want to see really honest objectives. You can't write: "I want an easy job that isn't boring, pays a lot, gives tons of time off, offers amusing co-workers and a pliable boss—to carry me through until my hit single takes off." And you can't write: "I don't know exactly what I want to do, but I thought I would try a job at your company to see if I like it."

So why have a job objective at all? Why should you have to make up a lie and risk not getting into heaven? Well, the fact is, *most resumes shouldn't include job objectives at all.* You've heard that every single resume absolutely *must* have a job objective at the top of the page? That's a myth. Most employers these days don't expect resumes to include job objectives; in fact, many think you shouldn't limit yourself by narrowing your options.

Job objectives evolved primarily as a convenience to personnel recruiters, who wanted to review stacks of resumes as quickly as possible. They function as screening devices, telling recruiters whether your goals match openings in their companies. If your objective perfectly reflects a current need, you get screened in. If you indicate a discrepant interest, you're eliminated. Unless you prepare a different objective for each job you apply for, your job objective will probably work against you.

Job objectives limit your options. If you state that you want to be a Senior Donut Packer, the recruiter won't consider you for that wonderful Bagel Rolling position in the Bread Department. And don't try to get around the dilemma by writing a wishy-washy job objective ("I'd like a growth position involving flour . . . "). You will look unfocused and unintelligent.

Instead of including a job objective in your resume, write a personalized, focused cover letter that indicates your interest in the particular position available. Don't worry about annoying recruiters by leaving off the objective. Nobody will reject you for lack of an objective if you have good credentials and a strong cover letter.

"Look—I didn't start out to become a volatile executive—I also thought about being a temperamental actor or a high-strung musician."

"BUT I'LL ONLY WORK AS A POODLE TRAINER IN A SMALL SALON," AND OTHER EXCEPTIONS

Does it *ever* make sense to have a job objective? Yes, if you have very specific job requirements and won't accept any other sort of work. Your job objective will prevent you from wasting time interviewing for jobs that don't really interest you.

Job objectives also make sense for career changers. The objective steers attention away from your background and emphasizes your new goals.

Finally, if you're a highly trained specialist and you like what you're doing, an objective can underline your commitment to your field.

WRITING AN EFFECTIVE JOB OBJECTIVE

You really need a job objective? Okay, but don't let that objective work against you.

The best job objectives tell both what you want to do *and* why you're qualified to do it. Your job objective can be a selling tool. For instance, instead of saying, "A position as a Bagel Roller," say, "A position as a Senior Bagel Roller using my five years of experience in all aspects of bagel production."

To be of any use, your objective must be specific. Tell exactly what you want to do, indicating the function, level, and environment you seek.

Use the worksheet on the next page to write your job objective.

WORKSHEET

Job Objective

Instructions: Select one of the job objectives below. Fill in the blanks and edit as you like. When you finish, copy your job objective onto your Resume Format Sheet.

1. An entry-level position as a _____ in a _____ (type of company) firm, using my degree in _____ and special training in _____.

2. A senior position in _____ (profession) using my _____ years of experience as a _____.

3. A _____ (type of job) position in a _____ (type/size) company, offering growth, and drawing on my considerable experience in _____.

4. A _____ (type and/or level of job) position in a dynamic nonprofit corporation, using my _____ expertise and _____ years of background in _____.

5. A growth position in a fast-paced _____ (type of company), using my _____ experience and allowing me to pursue my special interest in _____.

6. Write your own objective: _____
   _____
   _____
   _____

CHAPTER 4

GETTING IN THE SPOTLIGHT: SUMMARY OF QUALIFICATIONS, HIGHLIGHTS, AND SKILLS SECTIONS

"He who has a thing to sell
And goes and whispers in a well
Is not so apt to get the dollars
As he who climbs a tree and hollers."

—Anon.

After a full morning of faxing and bossing and memoing, employers don't want to read anything more complicated than "Peanuts." Too bad—they aren't allowed to read "Peanuts." Instead, they must shovel through mountains of paperwork from dawn to dusk.

How do they cope? By scanning. All documents that cross employers' desks get a 30-second once-over, except for truly interesting items such as lunch menus, cartoons, or offers of money—which get a more thorough reading.

No matter how striking your resume, to the employer it's just another ugly document with fine print and no pictures. You can bet it will go in the scan pile. But here's a special secret. After scanning, a few lucky documents move into that elite, inner circle of documents that *actually get read.* You want your resume to move into that inner circle? No need to attach cartoons or offers of money—instead, use a Summary, Highlights, or Skills section.

Spotlight sections appear at the top of the resume, above the Work History section. They emphasize your best qualifications, enticing employers to keep reading.

Note that you should use only *one* type of Spotlight section in your resume: Highlights, Summary, *or* Skills. How can you choose? Just follow the instructions below.

PICK YOUR BOAST

Virtually every resume benefits from a special Spotlight section. Like carefully chosen spice, a Spotlight section extracts and showcases the most delicious aspects of your resume, then adds a zing of extra flavor. Of course, you don't want to overspice your resume, so use only one type of Spotlight section. (Occasionally, a resume can use both a Summary plus either a Highlights or Skills section. Review the sample resumes in Appendix 2 for exceptions.) How do you know which to choose—a Summary statement, a Highlights section, or a Skills section? Follow these steps:

☐ 1. Go to the Checklist on page 20. Put a check mark next to each point that applies to you.

☐ 2. Go to the sample resumes in Appendix 2 and look for examples of each type of Spotlight section: Summary, Highlights, and Skills (also called "Areas of Expertise" and "Professional Expertise").

☐ 3. Based on both the Checklist and your review of the sample resumes, decide which type of Spotlight section you want to use.

☐ 4. Turn to the appropriate chapter and read it.
   Important Note. You might find the Worksheets for the Highlights chapter useful, no matter what type of spotlight you choose. Read them for inspiration. They begin on page 27.

   • "The Summary of Qualifications," Chapter 5, is on page 21.
   • "Highlights," Chapter 6, is on page 24.
   • "Skills," Chapter 7, is on page 32.

☐ 5. Complete the Worksheet at the end of the chapter you select.

☐ 6. Transfer the information from your Worksheet to your Resume Format Sheet.

☐ 7. Completed all the arduous steps above? Congratulations! You just finished writing the hardest part of the resume. By comparison, the rest of the resume will be a breeze. So give yourself a big reward. Clip the coupon on the next page and redeem it right now.

THIS COUPON ENTITLES BEARER TO ONE HOUR OF MINDLESS FUN. CHOOSE ACTIVITY FROM LIST BELOW:

☐ Watch cartoons or soap operas.
☐ Spend money on frivolous items.
☐ Eat Oreos or gummy bears.
☐ Read Kant.
☐ Snooze.
☐ All of the above.

Checklist

USE A SUMMARY OF QUALIFICATIONS IF

☐ You want to give an overview of your credentials, rather than cite particular skills or accomplishments.

☐ You have no room for Highlights because you have too much other information to pack in. Summaries take up less space than other types of Spotlight sections.

USE A HIGHLIGHTS SECTION IF

☐ You want to emphasize three or more particular accomplishments.

☐ You have strong work and/or academic background in your chosen field.

☐ You have impressive accomplishments in your chosen field.

USE A SKILLS/AREAS OF EXPERTISE SECTION IF

☐ You have a weak or unstable work history in your chosen field, but have the requisite skills to do a good job. Skills emphasize what you *can* do rather than what you have done.

☐ You want to show that you have abilities in several areas. For instance, if you have writing, teaching, *and* administrative skills, you can list skills for each of these areas.

☐ You have quite a few abilities NOT explicitly presented in the text of your resume. For instance, if you know particular computer languages and programs, various types of video production and editing equipment, or certain medical procedures and instruments—use this section to highlight your special knowledge.

CHAPTER 5

THE SUMMARY OF QUALIFICATIONS

"The best way to be boring is to leave nothing out."

—Francois Voltaire

A Summary of Qualifications contains a one- or two-sentence sales pitch highlighting your best credentials. It sits at the top of your resume, where it catches attention and knocks employers dead. That's the purpose of the Summary statement: to seduce readers right at the start with an elegant come-on.

Envision the poor employer—with migraine headache and post-lunch acid indigestion—facing a stack of three reports, 19 memos, and 50 resumes. Now imagine how you endear yourself when you communicate, in one easy-to-read sentence, the fact that you have the perfect qualifications for the job.

Ironically, the one-sentence version of your background probably sounds a lot better than the entire story. That's because a well-written summary, like a well-written murder mystery, reveals just enough to seduce readers, and at the same time, conceals enough to keep them entranced.

Take the case of Jo Jo, who wants a job as an editor for *Vogue* magazine. She currently sells crystals on Key West. Last year, she was the editor of a local newspaper. Before that, she was a secretary and writer of greeting card verse, and prior to that, was a scarf model at a fashion clothing store.

This is the Summary Jo Jo wrote: "Extensive experience in editing, writing, and fashion, with expertise in all facets of editorial production and a proven ability to handle massive amounts of administrative detail."

Jo Jo's Summary is both powerful *and* truthful. If she started her resume by describing her most recent position as a crystal merchant, employers wouldn't keep reading.

To compose your Summary statement, complete the worksheet on the next page. Feel free to alter the wording or to write your own summary.

WORKSHEET

Summary of Qualifications

Instructions: Select one of the summary statements below. Fill in the blanks and edit as you like. When you finish, copy the summary onto your Resume Format Sheet. Note that you can name the Summary section "Summary" or "Summary of Qualifications."

1. Over _____ years of experience as a _____, with specialized expertise (exceptional skills) in _____.

2. Highly skilled _____, with advanced training in the field of _____.

3. Award-winning _____, with outstanding record of accomplishment in (special expertise in) _____. Additional track record _____.

4. Recent cum laude graduate of the _____ (program) at _____ (school) with special training in _____ and experience as a _____.

5. Proven track record as a _____, with credits (accomplishments) including _____ and _____.

6. Successful track record as a _____, with special expertise in _____ and _____. Additional experience in _____.

7. Accomplished _____, with proven skills as a _____, and special interest in _____.

8. Professional _____, with significant experience working for major corporations as a _____.

9. Proficient _____, with extensive experience in multiple facets of the business including _____ and _____. Accomplishments include:

   * _____
   * _____
   * _____

10. _____ (profession), with record of success in multiple phases of the business, including _____ and _____.

CHAPTER 6

HIGHLIGHTS

JUICY HEADLINES LURE READERS

"Knowledge is little; to know the right context is much; to know the spot is everything."

—Hugh von Hofmannthal

You're standing in line at the supermarket when you see the headline: "Adam and Eve were Space Aliens!" You think, "how stupid!" even as you thumb through the paper trying to find out what the article says.

Intriguing headlines make you want to read more. Coming attractions make you want to see the movie. What does this have to do with your resume? Should you attach a juicy headline ("Man with Atomic Brain Desires Job"), or a home video showing some of your more endearing qualities? Of course not, unless you want to work for *The National Enquirer*. Otherwise, settle for the more subtle but equally effective alternative: insert a Highlights section.

Like MSG, Highlights sections showcase the most delicious items in your resume, then add an extra kick. (Unlike MSG, your Highlights section won't kill you or even get you high, although the name *is* **highlights**.)

The Highlights section sits at the top of your resume; lazy-eyed employers don't have to read far to find out how great you are. It contains three to seven bulleted points, nicely formatted, all describing your best qualifications. Even employers who flip through your resume at supersonic speed can't help noticing those bold bulleted points right up at the top.

Why bullets? A landmark discovery in Nineteen Twenty-Something revealed that the scanning eye prefers bulleted items to dense paragraphs. However, **don't** attach a round of ammunition to your resume. Corporate sophisticates use the word *bullet* to describe a little round dot preceding an important point, like this:

> • The corporate world loves to bullet.

Highlights often repeat information revealed later in your resume. That's okay—certain feats bear repeating. You want to make sure that employers get the point (you're perfect for their needs), even if you have to clobber them with the facts several times.

For instance, Lana Hoe, a Landscape Architect, won five awards that she describes later in her resume. Her Highlights section says:

> • Won numerous awards for outstanding residential landscapes, 1987–90.

Note the word *numerous*. It tells the truth, but adds a special zing. Certain key words elicit an aphrodisiac effect in employers; if you use those words, the employer automatically wants you. Peppering your resume with even a few of those magic words can make a tremendous difference. The Worksheet at the end of this chapter will help you to incorporate magic words into your Highlights section.

The Highlights section often summarizes information implied— but not explicitly stated—in your resume. Check this example from Ms. Hoe's Highlights:

> • Track record in successfully administering all aspects of high-end projects, from proposal writing to work crew supervision.

Can you guess the magic words? Did you say *track record* and *successfully*? Bingo! Go make yourself a cup of tea. Grab two cookies. Recline. You have no cookies? Okay, just recline. After resting or digesting, peek ahead at Lana Hoe's completed Highlights section:

> *HIGHLIGHTS:*
> • Over 10 years of experience in high-end residential landscape design.
> • Honors graduate of the Radcliffe College Landscape Design Program.
> • Numerous awards for outstanding residential design, including the *National Peace Garden Award*, 1990.
> • Proven expertise in Japanese Garden design.
> • Track record in successfully administering all aspects of projects, from proposal writing to work crew supervision.

Without reading anything beyond Highlights, the employer knows that Lana Hoe possesses all the requirements for the job, plus more. Her most impressive credentials, listed one after the other without any filler text, convey the impression of a real dynamo.

Who benefits from using Highlights? People with strong backgrounds in their chosen field. You can't showcase something irrelevant like your prowess as a beach bum or as a hitchhiker. You must have a good educational background or a strong work history or achievements in your field. If you're a career changer, a re-entering homemaker, underqualified, or have other special problems, a Skills section will probably work better for you than a Highlights section.

BE YOU EVER SO HUMBLE . . .

"All you need in this life is ignorance and confidence, and then success is sure."

—Mark Twain

Here's the problem: Most people, modest creatures that they are, don't think they have good credentials. "I have no achievements," they say, "that's why I can't write my resume." Or, "There ain't been no highlights in *my* career." Is that you? Okay, maybe you really don't have any highlights. On the other hand, perhaps you think your highlights have to be as majestic as Mt. Everest, and that scares you. Relax. Even little accomplishments can sound quite grand if presented correctly.

How do you know if you have any highlights worth listing? Think about the type of job you want. You want to be a bank manager? Okay, do you have previous experience as a bank manager? Yes? That's sure a highlight. If not, do you have previous managerial experience? Or extensive banking experience? How about academic training in finance and management? All those things are highlights. So is a history of enhancing customer satisfaction, reducing turnover, working for a big-name corporation, publishing articles or business pieces, getting promoted, or even maintaining a perfect attendance record.

The highlights you list in your resume should reflect the type of job you want. If you want to work as a research scientist, don't highlight your sales or supervisory experience; list your M.S. in Chemistry and your success as an intern in Dr. Primple's lab. For a sales job, don't showcase your administrative savvy; accent your record of accomplishment in sales and customer relations.

Fortunately, this book makes it a snap for you to write an effective Highlights section. The Worksheet on the following pages provides fill-in-the-blanks wording for Highlights *by seven general types of profession*. Just follow the Worksheet instructions, complete your Highlights, and transfer them to your Resume Format Sheet.

One important point: it helps to review your Highlights section after completing the rest of the resume. The process of writing will probably jog your memory, plus give you an overview of your credentials. You might find some forgotten gems to add.

WORKSHEET

Highlights

Instructions

☐ 1. Review the Generic Highlights below, filling in the blanks and circling any that apply to you. Then, go to the appropriate specialized category of Highlights (more than one may apply to you).

   • ***Clerical,*** below
   • ***Management,*** page 28
   • ***Service,*** page 29
   • ***Student/Recent Graduate,*** page 29
   • ***Technical,*** page 30
   • ***Arts,*** page 30
   • ***Sales,*** page 31

☐ 2. Fill in the blanks for any entries that apply to you; circle those that you want to use.

☐ 3. Transfer all of your circled Highlights to your Resume Format Sheet.

☐ 4. If you want to create additional Highlights, review the sample resumes in Appendix 2 for inspiration.

GENERIC HIGHLIGHTS

1. Consistently received highest evaluations from superiors for outstanding performance in _____.
2. Maintained perfect attendance record for _____ years.
3. Proven ability to complete all jobs on time and under budget.
4. Promoted _____ times in _____ years.

CLERICAL HIGHLIGHTS

1. Superior word processing skills, with knowledge of (programs) _____, _____, and _____. Typing speed is _____ wpm.
2. Facility with a wide range of computer programs, including (word processing, desktop publishing, graphics, spreadsheets, database, accounting, time management) software.
3. Expanded duties within _____ (months/years) to include (coordinating all travel arrangements, editing reports and proposals, conducting research on _____, organizing special projects such as _____, preparing budgets for _____).
4. Extensive background (proven ability to organize) successfully organizing (special events/conferences/workshops/meetings) for up to _____ people, including (overseeing facility and food arrangements, distributing materials to attendees, track-

ing attendance, writing minutes, making travel arrangements, managing budget, arranging press coverage).

5. Successfully developed and implemented (improved) information tracking systems that reduced backlog (increased efficiency) substantially.

6. Proven ability to coordinate complex administrative functions, including _____, _____, and _____.

7. Expertise in maintaining exceptionally accurate records and in coordinating massive amounts of paperwork.

8. Proven ability to purchase all supplies, maintain inventory, and assure proper functioning of equipment for high volume office.

9. Exceptional proofreading and editing skills, with particular experience working on _____ (reports/proposals/materials).

10. Expertise using a wide range of office equipment, including _____, _____, and _____.

MANAGEMENT HIGHLIGHTS

1. Expertise supervising, training, and evaluating up to ____ staff members.

2. Proven track record in reducing staff turnover by ____ percent by (improving morale, realigning job responsibilities/introducing innovative management style/reorganizing departments/adding training and incentive programs).

3. Experience overseeing all personnel recruitment for a ____-member staff.

4. Exceptional success in implementing innovative employee training programs (that resulted in a _____ percent increase in retention.)

5. Proven success in establishing all (revising) policies and procedures for a _____-member (department/company).

6. Successfully developed (and/or managed) operating budgets of up to $_____.

7. Proven ability to increase profit margin in (department/company) by up to _____ percent (through implementing _____).

8. Successful track record in motivating staff to succeed.

9. Track record in garnering substantial funding from (private/public) sources, with recent awards up to $_____ for _____.

10. Expertise (managing/coordinating) all administrative functions for (fast-paced, complex, specialized) operations employing up to _____ staff, including supervising staff, overseeing finances, coordinating daily operations, and ensuring profitability.

11. Proven ability to develop business from $_____ to over $_____ in _____ (months/years).

12. Exceptional success reversing trend of losses for (multiple companies) (type of) _____ company.

13. Expertise developing exceptionally effective new products (including _____ and _____) and marketing strategies that increased revenues by _____ percent.
14. Over _____ years of successful experience (managing/developing/implementing) _____ in a _____ environment.
15. Exceptional success in increasing (membership/client) base by up to _____ percent.

SERVICE HIGHLIGHTS
1. Specialized (expertise/training) in helping _____ to _____.
2. Highly effective (teaching/training) skills, supported by top evaluations from students and superiors.
3. Effective counselor, with special training in _____, and direct experience in _____.
4. Special (expertise/training) in _____ production, with outstanding skill in _____.
5. Proven ability to complete complex and demanding projects with small crews and limited equipment.
6. Broadbased knowledge of _____ (type of) equipment, including _____, _____, and _____.
7. Proven success in troubleshooting complex _____ (type of) problems, with special skill in _____.
8. Apprenticed for ____ years to _____, a top-ranked _____.
9. Completed specialized training in _____ at _____ (institution), receiving a _____ (degree/certificate) (with honors).
10. (Received numerous commendations for maintaining/Proven ability to maintain) excellent customer relations.
11. Track record in successfully organizing (and supervising) high-volume (kitchen/warehouse/shop) handling _____ merchandise.
12. Proven ability to complete all jobs on time and under budget.
13. Substantial experience administering a wide range of medical products to patients, with special expertise in _____ _____.
14. Considerable background teaching patients self-care techniques and use of medical products.
15. Track record of reducing _____ (type of) costs by _____ percent, by implementing more efficient _____.
16. Increased student retention by ____ percent through (introducing/changing) _____.

STUDENT/RECENT GRADUATE
1. Awarded _____ degree (with honors) in _____ (field), _____ (date).
2. Outstanding record in student leadership. Held these offices: _____,

_____, and
_____.

3. Awarded _____ (fellowship/honors) for outstanding performance in _____.
4. Graduated _____ (rank) in class of _____ students.
5. Completed _____-month internship in _____ (subject). Selected from a pool of _____ (number) students.
6. Performed extensive research on _____, (with particular attention to _____).
7. Wrote paper selected for publication in _____, on the subject of _____.
8. Work experience includes
_____.

TECHNICAL HIGHLIGHTS

1. Track record as effective (project leader/manager) with experience overseeing all aspects of product development from conception to shipping.
2. Broad expertise using a wide variety of systems, including
_____.
3. Extensive software knowledge, including _____
_____.
4. Successful track record in (software/systems) design, analysis, and documentation.
5. Designed state-of-the-art _____ for _____ that _____.
6. (Directed/Executed) ground-breaking (research/product development) on _____, resulting in _____.
7. Won _____ award for (work on/design of/performance in/research on) _____.
8. Extensive knowledge of government standards and compliance requirements for _____, with proven ability to bring company up to standard within ____ (months/years).
9. Extensive background analyzing _____, with special skill in _____.
10. Expertise with statistical analysis packages, including _____
_____.
11. Considerable expertise in maintenance and repair of _____, with specialized (training/skill) in _____.

ARTS HIGHLIGHTS

1. Received numerous honors for _____, including the _____ (prize/award).
2. Received _____ award for outstanding _____.
3. Numerous publications in (type of) _____ (magazines/journals/newspapers), with subject emphasis on
_____.
4. Author of _____ (number) books on _____.

5. Built client list from _____ (number) to _____ (number), including (major corporations such as _____ /small businesses/individuals). Growth due to outstanding reputation as _____.

6. Expertise with numerous graphics systems, including _____, _____, and _____.

7. Exhibitions in _____ (galleries/halls) throughout _____; consistently received critical acclaim.

8. Critically-acclaimed performances include _____ and _____, with award for _____ role in _____.

9. Extensive specialized training in the _____ (type) school of _____ (art-form); studied under _____ (name).

10. Produced over _____ highly (successful/effective/powerful) (videos, shows, movies, plays) on _____ (subject).

11. Created (innovative/successful) (marketing materials/promotional materials/toy designs/ _____ designs) that resulted in _____.

12. (Developed/Produced/Created) (layouts/designs/plans, photographs) for numerous major clients including _____.

13. Extensive knowledge of production equipment, including _____.

14. Proven expertise in (several/all) phases of industrial design, including _____, with specialized expertise in _____.

15. (Studied/performed) with (name) _____.

SALES HIGHLIGHTS

1. Proven ability to develop new regions, moving business from $_____ to $_____ in _____ (months/years).

2. Exceptional track record in expanding customer base from _____ to _____ within _____ (months/years).

3. Highly effective closer, with success rate of _____ percent.

4. Achieved top sales of all _____ (job category) from a pool of _____ (number), for _____ (number) (quarters/ years) out of _____ (number).

5. Proven ability to enhance customer relations through increased service and communication.

6. Won numerous awards for top performance, including _____ _____.

7. Ranked Number _____ (representative/manager/salesman/ salesperson), _____ (year).

8. Outstanding record includes increasing market share by _____ percent.

9. Track record of consistently exceeding sales goals by up to _____ percent.

10. Expertise delivering highly effective presentations to groups of up to _____.

11. Exceptional success in helping customers to develop custom products that meet their particular needs.

CHAPTER 7

THE SKILLS SECTION (AREAS OF EXPERTISE)

"You're aggressive, ambitious, money-oriented, able to influence people from all walks of life—in short, you're just the type of guy we need."

I'VE NEVER HAD A COOKING JOB, BUT I MAKE A GREAT SOUFFLE

Joe "Kingfish" Malone has a problem. After nine years as a license plate maker for a certain Missouri institution, he wants to return to his previous profession, selling pharmaceuticals. His resume can't describe his aluminum banging expertise; no drug company will hire him. What can he do?

Solution: Write a Skills section. Same goes for Jack Wicker, who slept through seven years of employment as a statistician, but avidly pursued his hobby of fishing and now wants a job managing a fish store. And Barb Lacey, who wants to show off her diverse talents in three areas of achievement—ranching, writing, and lobbying—in pursuit of a job as a ranch lobbyist.

Skills sections—also called "Areas of Expertise"—provide special needs help to those with problem backgrounds. The Skills section sits on top of the page (above the Work History section) and takes up lots of room, so employers don't notice much beyond. Scads of bullets bombard readers like a machine gun, killing any resistance to your application.

The Skills section usually has two or three subsections, each with three to seven bullets. Barb Lacey has three subsections: one for ranching, one for writing, and one for lobbying. The Kingfish has two subsections. Take a look at his Skills section:

AREAS OF EXPERTISE

Sales	• Generating leads using personal contact. • Offering sales presentations to individuals and groups. • Developing new territories, with proven ability to increase number of customers by 50 percent within three years. • Providing customer service, with track record in developing extremely loyal client base.
Pharmaceuticals	• Possess broad-based knowledge of amphetamines, muscle relaxants, and psychotropic medications. • Consulted numerous medical facilities on safe administration and side effects of barbiturates.

When employers read the Kingfish's Skills section, they assume it describes his *recent* background in pharmaceutical sales. He doesn't lie: he doesn't say, "Just yesterday, I sold 10 pounds of Lithium." His credentials look great for the job; he has all the requisite expertise. In fact, his skills outshine those of the competitors, so his resume goes in the "serious candidate" pile, even after the employer realizes that his career path hasn't exactly been sterling.

The Skills section often mixes genres, listing both skills and accomplishments. Skills describe your abilities; accomplishments tell what you've done with those abilities. For instance, swimming is a skill. Winning a swimming race is an accomplishment. Typing is a skill. Doubling your typing speed is an accomplishment.

Kingfish includes several accomplishments ("track record in developing extremely loyal client base," "Consulted numerous medical facilities on safe administration and side effects of barbiturates"), and also lists skills ("Generating leads using personal contact," "Offering presentations to individuals and groups").

Mixing genres allows people with few accomplishments to make the most of what they have, but it causes bad grammar. Each item in a bulleted list *should* start with the same type of word (all verbs in present tense, for instance). Since accomplishments come from the past and skills live in the present, this becomes impossible. For instance, look at this potpourri from Jack Wicker's resume:

Fishing Skills	• Threading worms on hooks • Ice-fishing, fly-fishing, deep-sea fishing • Able to cast line 30 feet even in high winds • Won best dressed fisher award, 1988

Can Jack improve his list? He could add the verb "Know" before the "Ice-fishing, fly-fishing, deep-sea fishing" entry, so that three of his four items would start with verbs.

If you run into this snag, don't worry. Just try to be as consistent as possible.

Here's another puzzler. How should you punctuate items in a bulleted list? Answer: If even one item in the list is a complete sentence, end every item in the list with a period. If the list has no complete sentences, don't punctuate any of the items.

Should you use a Skills section? Yes, if you have a problem background. Skills sections also work well for people with an *overabundance* of qualifications. People like Ms. Lacey, who can ranch and write and lobby. Also people like Marcus Rambite, a computer wizard who wants to list the languages, equipment, and software he knows. And Nancy Reflex, a nurse who wants to spotlight her skills in acute care, mental health nursing, and clinic administration.

If you want to list your achievements and abilities *by category*, you need a Skills section. If you want to emphasize a number of skills not otherwise obvious in your resume, you need a Skills section. And of course, if you have a ragged past, you need a Skills section.

To write your Skills section, complete the worksheet on the next page. You expect to agonize for hours thinking up skills? Nonsense. This book lets you dance through the process.

WORKSHEET

Skills

Instructions

☐ 1. Review the list of skill categories below circling any areas of expertise that apply to your background.

☐ 2. Add any particular skill areas you want to include. Every profession requires different areas of expertise, so you might have profession-specific skill sets to append. For instance, if you're a medical technician, you might add a category for Emergency Medical Procedures and another for Patient Relations.

☐ 3. Choose two or three categories that describe the areas of expertise you want to highlight. For instance, if you want a job in Nursing Administration, you might select Administration, Clinic Management, and Nursing.

☐ 4. Write the name of your first skill category on the next page. Then, answer the questions that follow. Your first skill area should be the one that most strongly reflects your career goals.

☐ 5. Enter your second skill category on the top of page 37, and your third on page 38. Answer the questions on each page.

☐ 6. Review your responses. For each skill category, choose the three to seven responses that describe your best abilities. Then, transfer each skill category, followed by your chosen skills for that category, to your Resume Format Sheet.

AREAS OF EXPERTISE:

Accounting	Editing
Administration	Educational Administration
Advertising	Electrical Engineering
Banking	Event Planning
Broadcast Management	Financial Management
Clinic Management	Financial Planning
Coaching	Fire Prevention
Collections	Fundraising
Computer Skills	Hardware
Conference Planning	Kitchen Management
Construction	Labor Relations
Curriculum Design	Languages
Customer Service	Law Enforcement
Design (specify type)	Library Expertise
Direct Service	Marketing

Mechanical Engineering	Software
Nursing (specify type)	Supervision
Office Management	Teaching
Personnel Relations	Technical Editing
Personnel Management	Technical Training
Project Management	Technical Writing
Promotions	Training
Property Management	Writing
Public Relations	_____
Repair (specify type)	_____
Research	_____
Retail Sales	_____
Sales	_____

Skill Category #1: _____

*Instructions: Answer each question below as it applies **to this skill area**. An example appears on the first line after each question.*

1. Name any special equipment you know how to use:
   * *Macintosh Computers and Software* (example) _____
   * _____
   * _____
   * _____
   * _____
   * _____
   * _____

2. List special procedures you can perform:
   * *Ghostwriting full-length biographies* (example) _____
   * _____
   * _____
   * _____
   * _____
   * _____
   * _____

3. List special products you can create or produce:
   * *Fine European pastries* (example) _____
   * _____
   * _____
   * _____
   * _____
   * _____
   * _____

4. List special training you received:
   * *Courses in radio broadcasting at National Broadcasting Institute*
   * _____
   * _____
   * _____

5. List abilities or attributes you have been commended for:
   * *Negotiating between hostile parties* (example)
   * _____
   * _____
   * _____

6. List attributes you appreciate in yourself:
   * *Stay calm under pressure* (example)
   * _____
   * _____
   * _____
   * _____

7. List new things you have learned in this skill area:
   * *On-line editing of help screens* (example)
   * _____
   * _____
   * _____

Skill Category #2: _____

Instructions: Answer each question below as it applies to this skill area. An example appears on the first line after each question.

1. Name any special equipment you know how to use:
   * *VU Meter* (example)
   * _____
   * _____
   * _____
   * _____
   * _____
   * _____

2. List special procedures you can perform:
   * *Diagnosing circuitry problems* (example)
   * _____
   * _____
   * _____
   * _____
   * _____
   * _____

3. List special products you can create or produce:
   * *Write diagnostic manuals* (example) _____
   * _____
   * _____
   * _____
   * _____
   * _____
   * _____

4. List special training you received:
   * *Courses in management and accounting at Yale University*
   * _____
   * _____
   * _____

5. List abilities or attributes you have been commended for:
   * *Superior public speaking skills* (example)
   * _____
   * _____
   * _____

6. List personal attributes you appreciate in yourself:
   * *Ability to make quick decisions* (example) _____
   * _____
   * _____
   * _____
   * _____

7. List new things you have learned in this skill area:
   * *Basic VCR repair* (example) _____
   * _____
   * _____
   * _____

Skill Category #3: _____

Instructions: Answer each question below as it applies to this skill area. An example appears on the first line after each question.

1. Name any special equipment you know how to use:
   * *Photo enlargers* (example) _____
   * _____
   * _____
   * _____
   * _____
   * _____
   * _____

2. List special procedures you can perform:
   * *Black-and-white film development* (example)
   * _____
   * _____
   * _____
   * _____
   * _____
   * _____
   * _____

3. List special products you can create or produce:
   * *Photo-screened t-shirts* (example)
   * _____
   * _____
   * _____
   * _____
   * _____
   * _____
   * _____

4. List special training you received:
   * *Numerous design courses at the DeCordova Museum*
   * _____
   * _____
   * _____
   * _____

5. List abilities or attributes you have been commended for:
   * *Strong writing skills* (example)
   * _____
   * _____
   * _____
   * _____

6. List personal attributes you appreciate in yourself:
   * *Able to perform multiple tasks simultaneously* (example)
   * _____
   * _____
   * _____
   * _____

7. List new things you have learned in this skill area:
   * *Transferring computer-generated images to clothing*
   * _____
   * _____
   * _____
   * _____

CHAPTER 8

WORK HISTORY

"Don't worry if your job is small,
And your rewards are few.
Remember that the mighty oak
Was once a nut like you."

—Anon.

Remember dozing through Zachary Taylor's presidency in American History class? Why couldn't you stay awake? Probably because your lessons concentrated on boring facts, like the date of Taylor's birth and the date of his death. Snooze material.

Was Zachary Taylor inherently boring? Not at all. He had all sorts of juicy weirdness, like a pathological addiction to war and a mainly celibate life. Unfortunately, your lessons focused on the wrong things.

Look at the job listings on most resumes. What do they emphasize? Dates and places, duties performed. Boring, snoring facts. No wonder employers hate resumes as much as they hated pop quizzes.

"Responsible for all worm-digging efforts. Under the direction of the Chief of Worms, trained night crawlers." You expect to get a job with prose like that? Okay, you aren't a worm professional, so you'd write something high-brow like, "Responsible for coordinating all discretionary funds. Under the direction of the Head of Accounting, trained bookkeepers."

A worm by any name gets rejected the same. If you want a job, you need to breathe life into your Work History section. How? First, jazz up any facts you must include—like the place you worked, your job title, details about your responsibilities—and make those facts more interesting. Then, divorce yourself from your job descriptions and start thinking about the juicy stuff. What did others say about your work?

What was the most fun project you worked on? What were you best at? What were you proudest of? Tell about these things and even comatose employers will take heed.

JAZZING UP THE FACTS

"I'm an Alcohol Quality Engineer, and I like my work."

Winston Snit "tells it like it is." From December of 1989 to April of 1990, he worked for the Doghead Company as a receptionist. Here's what he wrote in his resume:

12/89–4/90	**RECEPTIONIST** Doghead Co., 35 Fain St., Wamstown, KY

Winston states the facts clearly and accurately. Nothing to take issue with, right? Wrong! The truth can have many shades and in Winston's case, using a different hue makes much more sense.

What's the first thing you notice when you look at Winston's listing? Probably those ugly dates out in the left column. They look ghastly, plus they boldly advertise Winston's embarrasingly short tenure with Doghead.

If you intended to put *your* dates in the left column, think again. Employers read from left to right. Why put your dates first? Even if you stayed in your job for seven respectable years, your dates won't impress. Use the left column for your most impressive detail—either your job title or the company name. Stick those homely dates in parentheses on the right, like this:

RECEPTIONIST (1989–90)
The Doghead Company, Wamstown, Kentucky

Notice something missing? Where did Snit's months of employment go? To the land of nonessentials. You don't need to show the exact moment of your arrival and final departure from the job. If you list your dates of employment by year only, employers won't care, and your page will look much less cluttered.

Snit's problems don't end with his dates. His job title doesn't delight employers either. In truth, Winston's duties as a receptionist included writing proposals, supervising 10 clerical workers, and tracking thousands of dog bones each week. Not exactly typical duties for a receptionist. How can he get around his low-level title? Should he adopt a more accurate and impressive tag, like "Administrative Coordinator" or "Office Manager?"

It depends. If Snit's former employer doesn't care what he calls himself, Snit should adopt any title that accurately describes the highest-level work he performed. But if he can't get away with creating a new title, he should eliminate his job title entirely. Instead, he can list the name of the company he worked for and his department, like this:

THE DOGHEAD COMPANY, Wamstown, Kentucky
Bone Department (1989–90)

If your situation resembles Winston's but you *must* include your job title, at least hide it on the second line without bolding or underlining it.

The rules below summarize everything you need to know to format your Work History section:

WORK HISTORY FORMAT RULES

☐ 1. Start your Work History section with your most recent job. List previous positions in descending chronological order.

☐ 2. Don't list any jobs you held more than 20 years ago.

☐ 3. If you held important and relevant jobs more than 20 years ago and you really want to include them, summarize them at the end of your Work History section without including dates, like this:

Additional experience includes seven years as the Chief Tester for Cheap Thrills Yo Yos, Peoria, Indiana

---

☐ 4. If you held several part-time jobs simultaneously, avoid confusion by indicating that the positions were part-time, like this:

PARTY PLANNER (Part-time, 1982–88)
The Fun Chicken, Mudville, Alabama

BOUNCER (Part-time, 1983–87)
The Rowdy Rabbit, Teegsville, Alabama

☐ 5. Don't list the street address of the company you worked for, your supervisor's name or job function, or part-time jobs that have no relevance to your goals. Always avoid cluttering up your resume.

☐ 6. If you had a respectable, or even regal, job title, promenade it in bold. Let readers know in a big way that you were important, like this:

DIRECTOR OF EVERYTHING (1984–87)
Sandbag Play Time, Snailsville, Tennessee

☐ 7. If your job title doesn't convey the breadth of your duties and your former employer won't care what you call yourself, coin a title that accurately describes the highest-level tasks you performed.

☐ 8. If you can't get away with creating a new title, eliminate your job title entirely. Just list the name of the company you worked for and your department, if you had one.

☐ 9. Don't list dates of employment in the left column. Put them in parentheses to the right of your job title.

☐ 10. Don't include months of employment. List your dates of employment by year only.

POLISHING YOUR JOB RESPONSIBILITIES

"It says right here in your job description that Tuesday is your day to bring falafel."

Obviously, you got sick of your old job or you wouldn't have left it, right? It's hard to muster up enthusiasm for jobs you discarded long ago. But if you don't describe your past with some gusto, employers will feel the boredom in your prose. They'll lose interest in you. So fake it: use verbs.

Remember that old adage, "The verby bird gets the work"? In your Work History section, verbs count more than anywhere else in the resume. Every sentence after your job title/employer line should start with a verb. And not just any old verb—"Did laundry" doesn't have half as much impact as "Processed laundry." "Made peanut butter sandwiches" pales next to "Oversaw peanut butter sandwich preparation."

Look at the job description below:

> Involved in testing and producing gummy bears. Responsible for modifications. Worked from recipes.

Now look at this verby version:

> Managed production and testing of gummy bears. Introduced innovative modifications. Developed new recipes.

Observe the improvement? Sure you do. But you don't know how to transform your own resume with verbs, because you don't remember the parts of speech? Don't worry. The Worksheet at the end of the chapter includes a list of action verbs you can use. You'll find verbs for all occasions and vocations. Choose those you need and plug them right in.

TELLING THE JUICY STUFF

> *"My father taught me to work, but not to love it. I never did like to work, and I don't deny it. I'd rather read, tell stories, crack jokes, talk, laugh—anything but work."*
>
> —Abraham Lincoln

What's the most beloved word in employer-speak? "S-U-C-C-E-S-S." Employers pine for achievers—devoted workers who can solve pressing problems and leap tall buildings in a single bound.

Your work history has no high points? You have nothing great to show or to tell? Bah humbug! Of course you do. Everyone has achievements. Even you.

Stop whining about your plebeian past and go on an achievement hunt. Start by scanning your past for statistics, the second love of employers. You supervised employees. How many? You managed a budget. How large? You served customers. How many each day? You edited a famous book. How long did it take you?

Look at the gummy bear job description, improved now with statistics:

Managed production and testing of 79,000 gummy bear packages each month. Introduced innovative modifications. Developed 23 new recipes over a two-month period.

It's getting better all the time, right? But is it juicy enough yet? Not quite. After adding statistics, you still need to tell about your most outstanding feats. Some hot-shots have accolades and trophies to brag about. Others have more humble achievements, like improving the filing system, gaining a few customers, or arriving at work on time every day. Unless you got fired (legitimately) for poor performance, you undoubtedly did *something* right in your former jobs or you wouldn't have lasted. This is where to tell about it.

When boasting about your achievements, always discuss the results of your actions. When you modified the filing system, did you enhance efficiency in the office? Say so. Did your great attendance record reduce costs by reducing the need to hire temporary help? Did the customers you recruited result in increased revenues for your company? Tell all about it.

Look at the gummy bear job description now, complete with finishing touches:

PRODUCT DEVELOPMENT MANAGER (1984–87)
Great Gummies, Larchville, North Dakota

Managed production and testing of 79,000 gummy bear packages each month. Developed 23 new recipes over a two-month period.

Achievements

- Introduced innovative modifications that resulted in a 20 percent increase in sales.
- Wrote a gummy bear recipe booklet that received excellent reviews.
- Received superior performance evaluations every year.

You can bet employers will read your achievements before they read your job description. Remember, the scanning eye prefers bullets. So don't be modest in this section. What you write here can move your resume from the Land of Nod to the Kingdom of Employment.

The worksheet on the next page will help you identify your achievements and write a great Work History section. (Note that you can also call your Work History section "Professional Experience," "Employment History," or "Positions Held.")

Important Note: Do not proceed to the worksheet if you have any of these troublesome issues in your background:

- A job-hopping history
- No (or very little) work experience
- Too many years in the same job
- A recent career change
- Age over 50
- A long history of unemployment

Instead, turn to Chapter 15, "Special Problems," and read it now. After you finish Chapter 15, return to the worksheet on the next page and complete it.

WORKSHEET

Work History

You will build your Work History section step by step, starting with the heading for each of your jobs. Follow the instructions below:

STEP 1. FORMAT YOUR JOB HEADINGS

☐ 1. Decide which is more impressive: your job titles or the names of the companies you worked for. Go to your Resume Format Sheet. On the first line of each Work History block on your Resume Format Sheet, enter your most impressive detail. Be consistent: if you start one entry with your job title, you must start all other entries with your job title also.

☐ 2. Remember to start with your *most recent job*. List previous jobs in reverse chronological order.

☐ 3. If your job titles are on Line One, write the names and locations (town and state only) of the companies you worked for on Line Two. If your company names are on Line One, enter your job titles on Line Two.

☐ 4. Enter your dates of employment (years only) in parentheses to the right of your job titles.

☐ 5. Remember that job titles are optional. Don't use titles if they are less impressive than your experience.

Your completed job headings will look something like this:

PRESIDENT (1986 to 1989)
Duchess Gags, Shamram, Ohio

---

or

THE WHITE HOUSE, Washington, D.C.
Party Planner (1988–90)

STEP 2. WRITE YOUR JOB DESCRIPTION BLOCKS

☐ 1. Make a list of your responsibilities for each of your jobs, using the form below.

☐ 2. Make sure you start each responsibility with an action verb. Refer to the List of Action Verbs on pages 50 and 51 for help.

☐ 3. Review your list of responsibilities. Quantify each entry, wherever possible. For instance, if you wrote "Supervised staff," tell the number of staff you supervised, unless that number is unimpressive. Or, if you wrote "Served cus- tomers," add the number of customers you served on a busy day ("Served up to 80 customers a day").

☐ 4. Choose the most important and impressive responsibilities from your list. Using those responsibilities, compose a job description for each job. Try to limit length to five lines. Always start each job description with *the* most impressive responsibility and work backwards. Refer to the sample re- sumes in Appendix 2 for guidance.

☐ 5. Enter your completed job descriptions in your Resume For- mat Sheet.

Job Responsibilities

Most Recent Job

* _____
* _____
* _____
* _____
* _____
* _____

Previous Job

* _____
* _____
* _____
* _____
* _____
* _____

Previous Job

* _____
* _____
* _____
* _____
* _____
* _____

Previous Job

* _____
* _____
* _____
* _____
* _____
* _____
* _____
* _____

Previous Job

* _____
* _____
* _____
* _____
* _____
* _____

STEP 3. ADD ACHIEVEMENTS—THE FINISHING TOUCH

- [ ] 1. Answer the questions below for your two or three most recent jobs. You don't need to include achievements for previous jobs, unless you have the room and you want to.

- [ ] 2. Review your answers. Choose the most impressive responses, and rephrase each as an achievement. Remember to start each achievement with a verb. For instance, if your answer to Question 1 ("What were you proudest of?") was "I took over the responsibilities of the Dean for Student Affairs," your achievement would state "Assumed all responsibilities of the Dean for Student Affairs."

- [ ] 3. Transfer your achievements to your Resume Format Sheet.

- [ ] 4. How many achievements should you list? You need a minimum of one for each job; three to four are much better.

- [ ] 5. If you can't think of any achievements, refer to the sample resumes in Appendix 2 for inspiration.

Most Recent Job

Job Title: _____

1. What were you proudest of in this job? _____
_____

2. What did others commend you for? _____
_____

3. Did you get written or verbal commendation or excellent performance evaluations? (specify)
_____

4. Did you win any awards? _____
_____

5. What improvements did you make for your department or company?_____
_____

6. Did you increase efficiency, profits, or savings for your company or department? _____ How?
_____

7. Did you introduce any new procedures, programs, or materials? (specify)
_____

8. Did you reorganize anything? (specify) _____
With what results?
_____

9. Were you promoted? _____ How many times? _____ In how long? _____

Previous Job

Job Title: _____

1. What were you proudest of in this job?_____
_____

2. What did others commend you for?_____
_____

3. Did you get written or verbal commendation or excellent performance evaluations?

   _____

4. Did you win any awards?_____

   _____

5. What did you improve for your department or company?_____

   _____

6. Did you increase efficiency, profits, or savings for your company or department? _____ How?

   _____

7. Did you introduce any new procedures, programs, or materials? (Specify)

   _____

8. Did you reorganize anything? (specify)_____

   _____

9. Were you promoted? _____ How many times? _____ In how long? _____

Previous Job
Job Title: _____

1. What were you proudest of in this job? _____

   _____

2. What did others commend you for? _____

   _____

3. Did you get written or verbal commendation or excellent performance evaluations?

   _____

4. Did you win any awards? _____

   _____

5. What did you improve for your department or company? _____

   _____

6. Did you increase efficiency, profits, or savings for your company or department? _____ How?

   _____

7. Did you introduce any new procedures, programs, or materials? (specify)

   _____

8. Did you reorganize anything? (specify) _____

   _____

9. Were you promoted? _____ How many times? _____ In how long? _____

ACTION VERBS

Accelerated	Advised	Attained
Accomplished	Analyzed	Audited
Achieved	Applied	Augmented
Acquired	Appointed	Authored
Acted	Approved	Bought
Adapted	Arbitrated	Broadened
Addressed	Arranged	Built
Administered	Assessed	Centralized

Charted	Forecasted	Procured
Clarified	Formulated	Produced
Collaborated	Founded	Programmed
Completed	Generated	Projected
Composed	Guided	Proposed
Computerized	Hired	Proved
Conceived	Identified	Provided
Condensed	Implemented	Published
Conducted	Improved	Purchased
Consolidated	Improvised	Recommended
Constructed	Increased	Reconciled
Consulted	Influenced	Recorded
Contracted	Initiated	Recruited
Contributed	Inspired	Redesigned
Controlled	Instigated	Reduced
Converted	Instituted	Regulated
Coordinated	Instructed	Reorganized
Corrected	Insured	Represented
Created	Integrated	Researched
Cultivated	Interpreted	Resolved
Decreased	Interviewed	Restored
Defined	Introduced	Reviewed
Delivered	Invented	Revised
Demonstrated	Investigated	Revitalized
Designated	Launched	Scheduled
Designed	Led	Secured
Detected	Located	Set Up
Determined	Maintained	Solved
Developed	Managed	Sponsored
Devised	Marketed	Staffed
Diagnosed	Mediated	Stimulated
Directed	Mobilized	Strengthened
Discovered	Modified	Structured
Documented	Monitored	Studied
Earned	Motivated	Suggested
Edited	Negotiated	Summarized
Effected	Obtained	Supervised
Eliminated	Operated	Surveyed
Employed	Ordered	Tested
Enforced	Organized	Sold
Engineered	Originated	Solved
Established	Painted	Sponsored
Evaluated	Participated	Tailored
Examined	Performed	Taught
Executed	Pinpointed	Trained
Exercised	Pioneered	Translated
Expanded	Planned	Undertook
Expedited	Prepared	Unified
Extracted	Presented	Verified
Facilitated	Printed	Won
Financed	Processed	

CHAPTER 9

EDUCATION

"It is my wish that this be the most educated country in the world, and toward that end I hereby ordain that each and every one of my people be given a diploma."

Drawing by Handelsman; © 1972. *The New Yorker Magazine,* Inc.

"'Whom are you?' he asked, for he had been to night school."

—George Ade

After four years of partying, John Lander somehow managed to get his Bachelor's degree. He headed out into the world looking for a job, armed with a smug attitude, the degree, and a pathetic lack of work experience. He wasn't worried. After all, his was a *Harvard* degree, and everyone knows Harvard graduates get jobs in a snap. Right?

Alas, poor John. He wrote the "HARVARD" in big letters across his resume, but no employer took the bait. Why? Because under the word "Harvard," the page was barren except for a list of pizza delivery jobs. Employers shun inexperienced help, even when that help has Ivy League credentials.

Of course, education does count for something. Harvard impresses employers more than Chimichanga U, and Chimichanga U beats no college at all. But whether your education was Ivy League or little league, you must play it up in a big way to compete with candidates who have more experience than you.

It isn't enough to state, "I went to Clark University and graduated." Instead, you must sing the song of your educational exploits loudly, describing both your proud and your petty accomplishments. If employers see you were a go-getter on campus, they'll assume you have the right stuff to knock 'em dead at work.

The Worksheet at the end of the chapter will help you to compose a stunning education statement. Use these rules to guide you:

SEVEN VERY BORING, VERY RELEVANT RULES

1. If you have meager work experience, place the Education section on top of your resume, right under the spotlight section. If you have substantial work experience, Education should *follow* Work Experience.
2. List all schools you attended in descending chronological order, starting with the school you attended most recently.
3. Do NOT list the high school you attended, unless you had truly outstanding accomplishments in high school.
4. Include a list of your relevant courses only if you need to beef up your resume. If you want to list quite a few courses, add a special subsection called "Major Studies" *below* your Education section. In this section, you can also describe any special projects or research you completed (see sample Student Resume, page A-87).
5. You were President of the Rolling Eggheads Society? Captain of the Football Team? Add a section called "Leadership" or "Leadership Activities." List the organizations you belonged to, noting any offices you held or awards you won (see page 59).
6. List professional development seminars and workshops you attended at the end of your education section. You can add a statement like this:

> **NUMEROUS PROFESSIONAL DEVELOPMENT SEMINARS** sponsored by Michigan University and the Society for Technical Communications, 1978–87.

If you think listing the workshops individually will strengthen your application, do so, particularly if you lack a formal degree.

You can skip right to the Worksheet on page 57 if your educational career has nothing ugly to hide. But if you dropped out, switched schools several times, never went to college, or graduated before my grandmother was born, better read the rest of the chapter.

THE WISE DROPOUT NEVER TELLS

"Never learn to do anything. If you don't learn, you'll always find someone else to do it for you."

—Mark Twain's mother

"Tune in, turn on, drop out," said Dr. Timothy Leary in the late 1960s. His prophetic words established a new credo. Hip students everywhere quit school; only dorks plugged through until graduation. Who needed a degree?

Every fun fad gives way to darker days, and the roaring 60s eventually led to the M.B.A. 80s and 90s. Degrees became prerequisites even for typing and hamburger-flipping jobs. Today, most jobs require a degree.

What can you do? You're a Bachelor of Nothing and a Master of None: you have no degree. Should you make a big deal out of your high school education, listing your year of graduation and good report card grades? Should you tell about the one year at Hobookie State College, noting that you had to leave due to pregnancy? Or should you beg the army to take you, since nobody else will? No, no, no! Lack of education won't hamper your ability to get a good job, provided you have work experience and a little resume savvy.

Why do employers require a degree? Do they believe a degree prepares you for a job? Of course not. They know how useless their own degree is (doctors, lawyers, and a few others excepted). Employers just want to know that you had brains enough and backbone enough to sludge through four years of boring, tedious work. They figure if you made it through school, you'll survive in the company.

How can you show you have brains and gumption, though you lack a degree?

IF YOU HAVE NO COLLEGE AT ALL
1. Show your intelligence and perseverance by including a bulky Skills or Highlights section and a detailed Work Experience section listing achievements for each job.
2. Eliminate the Education section entirely from your resume, although you can list any in-service courses you took in a section called "Professional Training."
3. Don't list the high school you graduated from, or in any other way call attention to your lack of higher education.

If your work background looks strong enough, employers probably won't notice your lack of a degree. If they do, they won't care.

IF YOU HAVE SOME COLLEGE BUT NO DEGREE
1. On the first line, list the name of the college you attended. If you went for three or more years, list the dates of attendance. Otherwise, don't.
2. List your major (and minor, if you had one) next.
3. List honors you received, special achievements, or relevant courses you took on the third line.

Here's the Education listing of James Markey, a three-year dropout:

> NEW YORK UNIVERSITY, School of Liberal Arts (1979–83)
> **Major in Political Philosophy; Minor in Economics**
> *Dean's list all semesters; 3.3 average*

Sound good? Who would notice James didn't get the degree?

THE MULTI-COLLEGE DILETTANTE AND OTHER SPECIAL PROBLEMS

"A college education shows a man how very little other people know."

—*Farmer's Almanac*, 1963

Five schools in seven years, and you never got a degree? Don't think employers will marvel at your sense of adventure. Employers seek stable candidates who will never leave, who will support them on snow days and weekend days (if needed), in sickness and in health, forever and ever. Your prospects don't look great.

If you jumped around from school to school, list only your most recent institution (of learning, that is). Add the name of another school only if it strengthens your application—if your studies at one school supplement your studies at another (you majored in music at one school, counseling at another, and want to work as a music therapist).

Entirely omit your dates of your attendance if necessary. If your record of attendance looks like this: 1976; 1979; 1982–83; 1988–89—don't incriminate yourself. The same applies if you graduated more than 20 years ago. A graduation date of 1961 alerts employers to your age. Sadly enough, some employers do discriminate.

Here's one tricky thing you can do if your educational career spans many years. Include dates for something you achieved recently (Dean's List, 1991), without mentioning your actual dates of attendance. If you finally received a degree after many years, list only your date of graduation.

Use the worksheet on the next page to compose your Education section. When you finish, transfer the information to your Resume Format Sheet.

WORKSHEET

Education

Instructions: Review the rules below. Then turn the page and review the sample Education statements. When you finish, fill in the blanks and choose the appropriate responses from the questions that follow. Don't worry if an entry doesn't apply to you. Simply complete the entries that do apply to you, then transfer the information to your Resume Format Sheet.

Remember

1. If you attended a prestigious school, list the school name (capitalized) on the first line. Otherwise, list your degree (capitalized) on the first line.
2. List your most recent school first. List preceding schools in descending chronological order. Don't include your high school.
3. Summarize your professional development courses at the end of the Education section, as described on page 53.
4. If you want to list courses you took, add a separate section and call it "Major Studies." List only your most relevant courses plus special projects or research you completed.
5. If you were active on campus, add a separate Leadership Activities section, noting offices you held or awards you won. This applies only to recent graduates. Others should incorporate leadership information right into their regular Education section.
6. Thinking about school requires extraordinary mental exertion. You'll need a little snooze to recover. If you can't sleep, read *Principles of Accounting* from cover to cover.

Sample Education Statements

Use these sample Education statements to guide you as you fill in the information for your Education statement on the next page:

UNIVERSITY OF MICHIGAN, Ann Arbor, Michigan ◄	——Line 1
Bachelor of Science in Biology, 1984. Minor in Psychology. ◄	——Line 2
Dean's List five semesters. 3.3 average in major courses. ◄	——Line 3

CERTIFICATE IN FINE PASTRY
The Genoise School, Paris, France
Special studies in puff pastry and croissant. Apprenticed under Chef Geoff Portnoy.

> SMITH COLLEGE, School of Social Work, Northampton, MA
> **Master of Social Work**, 1979. Emphasis on Family Systems.
> *Thesis: "Anger and Control in Single Parent Households"*
>
> - Received Alice Brown Fellowship. Chosen out of pool of 205.
> - Selected keynote speaker for Commencement, 1979.

Education Statement

Fill in the blanks and choose the appropriate responses. Remember that Line 1 and Line 2 are interchangeable.

Your Most Recent School

   1. Line 1. School Name: _____, (city and state) _____

   2. Line 2. Your Degree: (Certificate/Associate/Bachelor/Master/Doctor) of _____ in _____, 19____ (*optional*). (Major/Concentration/Emphasis) in _____. Minor in _____. (*If you can't fit all this on line 2, include it in line 3 below.*)

   3. Line 3. Graduated (Magna/Summa) cum Laude. G.P.A. (*if above 3.0*): ____. Dean's List ____ semesters.

   4. Line 4 and beyond. Check any accomplishments in the list below that apply to you. Write additional accomplishments in the blank spaces provided. Transfer your accomplishments to your Resume Format Sheet, listing each with an asterisk preceding it.

☐ • Received special honors or awards (specify)
☐ • Appointed to teaching assistantship or other special position
☐ • Achieved a high grade point average in major subjects
☐ • Selected for year abroad exchange program
☐ • Received scholarships or fellowships
☐ • Worked way through school
☐ • Graduated early
☐ • Studied with renowned people in field
☐ • Held leadership positions
☐ • Completed thesis/dissertation on (specify subject)
☐ • Ranked ____ in class of ____

* _____
* _____
* _____

Your Previous School

   1. Line 1. School Name: _____, city and state _____.

   2. Line 2. Your Degree: (Certificate/Associate/Bachelor/Master/Doctor) of _____ in _____, 19____ (*optional*). (Major/Concentration/Emphasis) in _____. Minor in _____. (*If you can't fit all this on line 2, include it in line 3 below.*)

3. Line 3. Graduated (Magna/Summa) cum Laude. G.P.A. (*if above 3.0*): _____. Dean's List _____ semesters.

4. Line 4 and beyond. Check any accomplishments in the list below that apply to you. Write additional accomplishments in the blank spaces provided. Transfer your accomplishments to your Resume Format Sheet, listing each with an asterisk preceding it.

- ☐ • Received special honors or awards (specify)
- ☐ • Appointed to teaching assistantship or other special position
- ☐ • Achieved a high grade point average in major subjects
- ☐ • Selected for year abroad exchange program
- ☐ • Received scholarships or fellowships
- ☐ • Worked way through school
- ☐ • Graduated early
- ☐ • Studied with renowned people in field
- ☐ • Held leadership positions
- ☐ • Completed thesis/dissertation on (specify subject)
- ☐ • Ranked _____ in class of _____

* _____

* _____

Previous Education and Professional Development Courses.

_____

_____

_____

_____

CHAPTER 10

PERSONAL INTERESTS/ACTIVITIES

"And in my spare time, I read Plato and ponder on the meaning of life."

At 3:00 on Friday afternoon, employees everywhere get happy. Impending fun looms in the office air, rendering most workers entirely useless. When the gong strikes five, a frantic exodus occurs. Mean-faced commuters honk and snort, desperate to get home to freedom.

We love our days off. Nothing beats time to play and dream; certainly not work. Oh, a few lucky souls combine avocation with vocation, but most folks pursue their passions only on nights and weekends.

So should you let a future employer know that you love to weave and to ski and to examine rare reptile droppings? If you mention that you rank as a national expert on reptilian behavior, will the employer think you lack career focus, or worry that you'll spend work time thinking about iguana life? Will including a Personal Interest statement help or hinder you?

"Personal interests have nothing to do with business, and don't belong on a resume," says the conservative voice of reason. Many vocational counselors agree. But in fact, most employers want to know what type of person you are.

Sure, employers wear suits and act boring. But under those suits and bland expressions, employers are real people who pursue fun with the same passion as you do. They don't want to hire some drippy nerd who has no life-energy. Given two equally qualified candidates, employers will choose the person who ran six marathons and shares their love for tap dancing.

Surveys reveal that employers like Personal Interest statements. Some old windbags find them offensive, but why work for someone who cares nothing for your fun side anyway?

ALL INTERESTS ARE NOT EQUAL

"When I see hobbies and crafts on a resume, I throw up. Everyone lists the same things: swimming, reading, and music. If they said, 'swimming, reading, and insects,' maybe I'd pay attention."

—Ray Barron, *President of Barron Hillman Mellnick, Inc., Boston, MA*

A word of warning. Don't include an interest statement if you have no interesting interests. Look at the statement below:

Personal Interests: Reading and cooking and sewing.

What type of person do you think wrote that? Someone passive and boring, right? Now look at those same interests, dressed up in more specific language:

Personal Interests: Detective novels, gourmet Thai cookery, and costume-making.

Who sounds like the more creative person? Who would you interview first? You hate detective novels and Thai food, so you'd prefer the no-personality nebbish? Okay, it's true: whenever you reveal your interests, you risk alienating some readers. But do you really want to work for someone totally unfriendly to your passions? Be specific in stating your interests. You will sound more interesting.

When employers read your Interest statement, they look for three things. First, are your interests similar to theirs? If so, they'll subconsciously favor you. "Oh, this person loves ice fishing and so do I. Oh gosh, he won the Big Hoe Ice Fishing Competition last year. He must be quite a person. I'll hire him." That's the way the subconscious mind works. If you mention interests that employers don't share, they probably won't care—unless you love something they absolutely hate, and that's the risk you run.

Employers also want to know if your personality fits the job. Do librarians need the same type of personality as car salespeople? Of course not. Would you interview someone who lists "hockey, car racing, and shark fishing" for a job as a librarian? Or someone who enjoys "reading, quiet walks in the woods, and birdwatching" for a car sales position? Hardly. Your Interest statement should support the type of work you want.

In general, employers prefer dynamic, interesting, gregarious types of people. They want to be sure that you won't sleep on the job and that you won't lull co-workers or clients to sleep either. If your interests read like a dirge, leave them out or throw in something a little more lively—unless you seek totally passive work.

Finally, employers want to make sure you aren't involved in anything weird. If you make cherry bombs in your spare time, campaign for the Bloody Toes Liberation Army, or preach for the Gates of Hell Wicca Club—few employers will want you. Never list really bizarre involvements unless you don't want a job. You should also avoid listing political or religious affiliations. On the other hand, if you feel very strongly about your controversial activities and don't want to work for anyone who can't accept them, go right ahead and list them. You may lose some interviews, but once you're hired, you won't have to stay in the closet.

BOWLING WITH A TWIST

"We need to reduce stress, men. That's why I'm mandating a half-hour of Tai Chi exercise every morning, starting now."

Brag, brag, brag—even in your Personal Interest statement. If your softball team ranks first in the league, if you completed a marathon or organized a major event, let readers know. You won bowling trophies or the Betty Crocker bake-off? You're treasurer of the Kennel Club, first soprano in the Chill Street Choir, coordinator of the Annual Fund Drive? Make a big splash about it. Employers know that if you excel in one area of your life, you have what it takes to excel in other areas as well.

Always list your extracurricular achievements, even if those achievements date back many years. Leadership positions held, awards won, activities initiated, athletic accomplishments—all deserve special mention. If you have a really astounding accomplishment—like winning an Olympic Medal or a Guinness World Record, mention it in your Spotlight section as well.

The worksheet on the next page will help you to write a tantalizing Interest statement.

WORKSHEET

Interests/Activities

Instructions: Review the Checklist and the sample Interest statements below. When you finish, fill in the blanks and compile your Interest statement. Note that you can call this section "Personal Interests," "Activities," "Interests," "Interests and Activities," "Volunteer Activities," or "Community Activities."

CHECKLIST

☐ 1. Include at least one *active* interest in your list. For example, instead of "Enjoy Theater," write "Enjoy acting in community productions."

☐ 2. Match your interests to the job you want. If you seek employment in an aggressive industry, show aggressive interests. If you want a position requiring public contact, show social interests.

☐ 3. Don't include controversial interests or interests indicating your religious affiliation or political preferences.

☐ 4. Don't list travel as an interest. Employers will worry that you'll take endless vacation time. But if you lived in another culture for an extended period, say so, especially if relevant to your goals. Also mention fluency in other languages.

☐ 5. Keep your Interest statement short, unless you have an outstanding record of accomplishment in your extracurricular life.

☐ 6. List your special accomplishments, or any leadership positions you held.

☐ 7. All this talk about interests has put you in the mood for play? Take a 10-minute joke break. Read a joke book or tell funny stories. Don't come back until you laugh.

SAMPLE INTEREST STATEMENTS

For an editing job:

Enjoy linguistics, photography, stamp collecting, and wilderness canoeing.

For a teaching job:

---

* Volunteer troop leader, Boy Scouts Troop 13, 1979 to Present
* Coach, Wackrack Little League. ***Won League Championship, 1987–90.***
Enjoy sailing, furniture restoration, and ham radio.

For a stockbroker job:

---

* Avid squash player.
* Won five medals for ski racing, 1985–88.
* Amateur stand-up comic. Major performances include ***The Comedy Shack***
and ***The Laugh Pit,*** both in Dallas, 1990–91.

NOW COMPOSE YOUR INTEREST STATEMENT

Fill in the blanks below. When you finish, review your entries and put an asterisk in front of each "active" (as in "dynamic") interest.

1. What hobbies have you pursued in the past 15 years?

   _____

   _____

   _____

   Special achievements or offices held:

   _____

   _____

2. What sports or physical activities have you participated in?

   _____

   _____

   _____

   Special achievements or offices held:

   _____

   _____

3. What adult education or special interest courses have you taken?

   _____

   _____

   _____

   Special achievements or offices held:

   _____

   _____

4. What musical, artistic, or creative endeavors have you participated in?

   _____

   _____

   _____

Special achievements or offices held:

_____

_____

5. What community or recreational organizations have you belonged to?

_____

_____

_____

Special achievements or offices held:

_____

_____

6. List your volunteer activities (teaching, coaching, collecting funds, organizing events, etc.).

_____

_____

_____

Special achievements or offices held:

_____

_____

7. List any other interests or activities.

_____

_____

_____

Special achievements or offices held:

_____

_____

8. Now compile your Interest statement. Choose the most relevant responses from questions 1–7 above. Remember to keep your Interest Statement short. Refer to the examples on pages 63 and 64 for guidance. When you finish, transfer your Interest Statement to your Resume Format Sheet.

_____

_____

_____

_____

_____

CHAPTER 11

REFERENCES

"Of every 10 persons who talk about you, nine will say something bad, and the 10th will say something good in a bad way."

—Antoine Rivaroli

You ooze charm and intelligence for a whole sweaty hour, then the interviewer calls your bluff. "I'd like to check some references," he says, looking at you expectantly. Your mind races wildly over the wasteland of your former jobs. "Who will speak for me?" you wonder, reflecting on the lazy days and nasty deeds behind you.

To avoid the last-minute reference showdown, some people list names and numbers of references right on their resume. This gives them plenty of advance time to scrounge up people who still like them. It also lets them name drop, in case they happen to know any big shots.

In spite of these advantages, avoid listing references on your resume. Why should you let employers nose around and talk behind your back before they even meet you? Do you want everyone who sees your resume to call your references and annoy them with probing questions? Until employers consider you a final candidate, don't let them burden your few admirers with a time-consuming interrogation.

The accepted practice these days is to write *"References Provided Upon Request"* across the bottom of your resume. This lets employers know that you're willing to provide references if asked for them. You can hope the employer doesn't ask, but for your own peace of mind, you should prepare a written list of references to take with you just in case. For more information on References, see Chapter 17.

All of the Resume Format Sheets in this book already say "References Provided Upon Request" across the bottom, so you don't need a worksheet.

CHAPTER 12

RESUME FRILLS: PUBLICATIONS, AWARDS, CERTIFICATIONS, AND MORE

"I haven't actually been published or produced yet. But I have had some things professionally typed."

Which sandwich would you grab: the one with pickle and chips on the side, or the unadorned one? Admit it—you'd take the pickle-chip plate. By comparison, the other looks like a gyp. We all want a little extra for the price.

Should you enclose pickles and chips with your resume, then? Of course not. Instead, you can add special frills. Resume frills satisfy the employer's hunger for "a little extra," but don't smell as bad as pickles.

RESUME FRILLS

Resume frills can include lists of:

- Honors and awards you won
- Professional organizations you belong to
- Things you published
- Speeches you gave
- Certifications or special licenses you possess
- Exhibitions or performances
- Public offices you held
- Clients you worked with

Most people don't have frills to flaunt. That's okay. A no-frills resume does just fine if garnished with a strong Spotlight section and good formatting. But if you do have frills, tout them like anything—they definitely enhance your resume.

SHOULD YOUR FRILLS STAND ALONE?

You can often blend frills right into the text of the resume. For instance, if you gained teaching certification along with your degree, you can list the certification in your Education section. If you published an article about teeth while working for a dentist, you can list the article in your Work History section.

When is a special frills section necessary? When you have an overabundance of frills. For instance, if you have 15 publications, you need a special place to showcase them. If you won seven awards, you need a special "Honors and Awards" entry. To describe your 20 exhibitions, you need a special "Exhibitions" entry.

You also need a frills section if you have activities and accomplishments that don't logically fit in any other section. And, you need a frills section if you want to make a big deal out of things that might otherwise get lost in the body of your resume. For instance, if you belong to several professional organizations and don't want to hide them in your Activities section, you can create a special section called "Professional Organizations."

Where should you stick your frill? It depends. Usually the frill section follows Education and precedes Interests/Activities. But if you have an abundance of honors and awards, your special Honors section should sit right at the top of your resume, substituting for the Spotlight section.

Major achievers of the Einstein-type may run out of room for their frills in a two-page resume. If you have long lists of publications or exhibitions or other hot-shot endeavors, you need to create separate attachments to your resume. Don't increase your resume beyond two pages. (Academic resumes—Curriculum Vitae—are an exception. They can exceed two pages.) Instead, create a separate page for your list of great deeds and attach it to your resume.

FOR AUTHORS ONLY

"I don't care what people think of my poetry so long as they award it prizes."

—Robert Frost

You wrote a big-shot book and a coherent article? Of course you're proud. Of course you should get hired before anyone else in the world, at an astronomical salary. But unfortunately, your illiterate listing of your publications makes everyone laugh. "She wrote a book and doesn't know that a comma should come after the publisher's name?" they snicker. Don't let them humiliate you. Learn these simple format rules now.

BOOK FORMAT

Italicize or underline the name of the book. Follow with a period, then place of publication followed by a colon. Then publisher, followed by a comma and the date of publication, like this:

Dorky Days and Nerdy Nights. New York: Bleck Publishing House, 1991.

If you co-wrote your book with another person, you must start the entry with the authors' names (Milton, John, and Flo Smacker.) followed by a period.

ARTICLE FORMAT

Start with the name of the article in double quotes, followed by a period. Then list the name of the periodical, italicized, followed by a comma and the date of publication, again followed by a comma. End with the page numbers, like this:

"My Mother Dated a Cow." *Ranch Life*, 13 August 1974, pp. 22–27.

Use the worksheet on the next page to compose your Frill sections.

WORKSHEET

Resume Frills

Instructions: Fill in the blanks for each frill section that applies to you. When you finish, transfer the information to your Resume Format Sheet. Attach additional sheets if necessary.

HONORS AND AWARDS

1. Awarded the _____ (Prize/Award/Medal) by _____ for _____, 19_____.
2. Named Honorary _____ by the _____ _____ for _____, 19_____.
3. Won _____ place in the _____, 19_____, for _____.
4. Received the following honors:
   • _____, 19_____
   • _____, 19_____
   • _____, 19_____
   • _____, 19_____
   • _____, 19_____
   • _____, 19_____
   • _____, 19_____
5. Additional honors

   _____
   _____
   _____
   _____

PROFESSIONAL ORGANIZATIONS/PUBLIC OFFICES HELD

1. Member, (*Organization Name*) _____, (*Location*) _____, 19_____ to 19_____.
2. (Elected/Appointed) (President/Vice-President/Secretary/Treasurer/Chair) of the _____, (*Location*) _____, 19_____.
3. Served as (*position/title*) _____ for the (*Organization Name*) _____, (*Location*) _____, 19_____ to 19_____.
4. Additional organizations/offices

   _____
   _____
   _____
   _____
   _____

PUBLICATIONS

If you have extensive publications in various media, subdivide this section into Books, Periodicals, Software, and so on.

1. (*Book name*) _____.
   (*Place of Publication*) _____:
   (*Publisher*) _____, 19____.
2. (*Article Name*) "_____."
   (*Periodical Name*) _____,
   (*Date*) _____, pp. ____–____.
3. (*Authors' Names*) _____ and
   _____. (*Book Name*)
   _____. (*Place of Publication*)
   _____: (*Publisher*) _____,
   19____.
4. (*Authors' Names*) _____.
   (*Article Name*) "_____."
   (*Periodical Name*) _____,
   (*Date*) _____, pp. ____–____.
5. Additional publications:

   _____
   _____
   _____
   _____
   _____
   _____
   _____
   _____

PRESENTATIONS/EXHIBITIONS/PERFORMANCES

1. (Keynote/Invited/Guest) (Speaker/Panelist/Lecturer),

   _____,
   (*Location*) _____, 19____.
   Subject: _____.
2. Performances Include:
   - (*Place*) _____, (*Role or*
     Composition) _____, 19____.
   - (*Place*) _____, (*Role or*
     Composition) _____, 19____.
   - (*Place*) _____, (*Role or*
     Composition) _____, 19____.
3. Exhibitions of Work Include:
   - (*Place of exhibition*) _____, (*Title of Work, or type*
     of exhibit) _____, 19____.
   - (*Place*) _____, (*Title or Work, or type of*
     exhibit)_____, 19____.
   - (*Place*)_____,
     (*Work*) _____, 19____.
5. Additional presentations, exhibitions, or performances:

   _____
   _____
   _____
   _____
   _____
   _____
   _____
   _____

CERTIFICATIONS/LICENSES
Hold the following (certifications/licenses):

* _____ , (*location*) _____ , 19____
* _____ , (*location*) _____ , 19____
* _____ , (*location*) _____ , 19____

CLIENTS
Client list includes:

- (*CLIENT NAME*) _____ ,
  (*Location*) _____ (19____ to 19____).
  (*Project*) _____
- (*CLIENT NAME*) _____ ,
  (*Location* _____ (19____ to 19____).
  (*Project*) _____
- (*CLIENT NAME*) _____ ,
  (*Location*) _____ (19____ to 19____).
  (*Project*) _____

PART 2

FINE TUNING YOUR RESUME

CHAPTER 13

RESUME NO-NOs

VITAL STATS

You won the Fishy Waters Beauty Pageant last month, and now you want to advertise your great looks. Should you attach your photo to your resume? Should you indicate your height, weight, and marital status in case someone wants to ask you out?

Years ago, all resumes included nosy personal information like eye color, names of pets, and other vital statistics. Now, Affirmative Action laws prohibit employers from weighing such information into their hiring decisions. Except for the gauche and the ignorant, nobody reveals personal statistics anymore. And absolutely nobody attaches photos to their resumes, except maybe actors, models, and others in professions where appearance directly affects performance.

Save your photo and your grandchild's name for the family reunion. In the business world, such information no longer wins jobs.

MONEY, HONEY

Here's another puzzler. Should you give your salary history, or tell how much money you want to make? Absolutely not! Listing salary requirements in a resume is as silly as telling your boss what you *really* think of her haircut. Neither action will accelerate your career.

Remember, your resume must drip with dignity. Mentioning money or other confidential matters breaches the royal code of resume pomp. Anyway, why screen yourself out by indicating that you want more money than employers want to pay? After they meet you, they may decide to cough up more than they originally intended.

What if an employer asks you for your salary requirements? Play cagey. On your cover letter, write "Salary requirements negotiable, depending on responsibilities and other compensation." If you absolutely *must* give a salary history or salary requirements, do so in your cover letter, not on your resume.

EXOTIC TOUCHES

You want your resume to attract attention? Printing it on flaming red paper will do the trick—if the type of attention you want is laughter and ridicule. Think about it. What do employers wear? Gray suits, navy blue suits. Colors that resemble mourning colors. Why? Because employers fear flash and glitter. They don't want to be reminded that a world of fun exists outside the office confines. So never print your resume on fun colors—stick to conservative whites, off-whites, and light grays.

What about poster board, oversize paper, resumes in tubes or on video? How about the pamphlet-style resume?

Forget it. Employers seek people who blend in; they don't want any troublemakers on board. Sure, they want you to be a little smarter than average and to have some creativity, but nothing outside the norm.[1] Your eccentric resume tells employers that you don't agree with the established way of doing things. And who determines the established way of doing things? The employer, of course. Renegades need not apply.

DO YOU LABEL YOUR FACE?

Never write the word "Resume" across the top of your resume. Do you label your face? Do you wear a sign around your neck saying "Human Being"? Of course not. Everyone knows what you are, assuming you are, in fact, human.

Your resume doesn't need a label either. Employers know what a resume is.

THE BIGGEST NO-NO OF ALL

Can you spell typo? Employers want efficient, accurate, trustworthy employees. If you send a resume with misspelled words, typos, smears, or dog ears, you'll evoke instant animosity.

Send a clean, current copy of your resume, with no handwritten insertions or commentary in the margins. Make sure everything is spelled correctly, including the employer's name on the cover letter. If you can't proofread well, hire a greedy friend to do it for you.

---

[1]A few professions—such as graphic arts and advertising—actually welcome creative resumes. They are rare exceptions.

CHAPTER 14

MAKING YOUR RESUME LOOK BEAUTIFUL

"It is only shallow people who do not judge by appearances."

—Oscar Wilde

An ugly resume is like a person with bad breath. Nobody wants to get near it, even if it says great things. To make employers see rainbows and hearts, you need a beautiful resume.

Should you paint a lovely border around the edges of your page? Should you add glitter or a splash of cologne? No, no, no. In resume design, understated elegance always wins.

Here are some pointers:

RESUME HYGIENE

Remember that wise old maxim: cleanliness is next to jobliness? A resume with smears, dog ears, or spaghetti splatters will land in the trash can. Don't think employers won't notice your erasures or grease spots. Toss your blemished resume and make a clean copy.

PAPER

Would you go to a wedding in a flimsy, cheap rag? Of course not. You know that everyone judges you by your appearance, and rightly so. In the same way, your resume must project breeding and class. Nothing ruins a perfectly good resume more quickly than chintzy paper and tacky type.

Print your resume on good quality paper. **Don't** use erasable bond or cheap copy stock. Use paper that looks important—preferably 24-pound linen or bond with a watermark. **Don't** use anything shiny or slippery. You want a paper that will feel substantial in the employer's hands.

Most print shops have a good selection of papers. Ask for help.

When picking out paper color, remember that employers don't want glamour on the job. Disregard your chartreuse or aqua tastes and go for white, off-white, or light gray.

TYPEFACE

Using bad typeface is like getting a bad haircut. It may be convenient and cheap, but you come off looking like a dog. It's worth the extra money and effort to have your resume typed nicely.

Resume typeface *must* be clear, sharp, and large enough to read without squinting. If you type your own resume, use a modern typewriter with film ribbon, or a letter-quality computer printer. Otherwise, have your resume typeset.

Avoid script styles or anything fancy. Also avoid blocky, heavy typestyles. Use standard 10- or 12-point fonts such as Times Roman, Helvetica, or Courier.

LAYOUT

You want the charismatic, super-rich Dr. Digital to notice you. Do you bury yourself in a crowd? Not you. Instead, you stand alone on a stool, singing the *Carmina Burana* loudly. Anything for attention.

In the same way, your credentials need space to shine, *so don't crowd your pages*. If you leave ample white space, important points will jump out at readers.

Smart resumes have hefty margins, and lots of room between blocks of text. Margins should be at least one inch on all sides. Double space (or more) between job listings; triple space (or more) between categories of information.

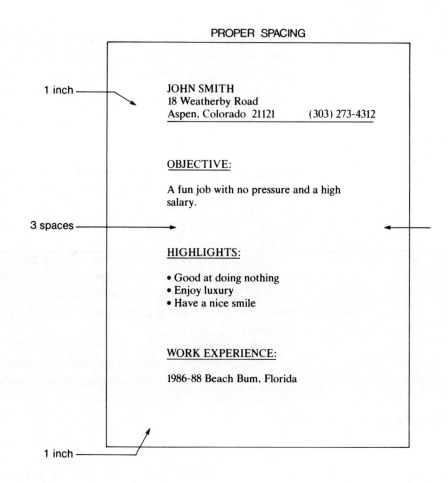

PROPER SPACING

1 inch →

JOHN SMITH
18 Weatherby Road
Aspen, Colorado 21121   (303) 273-4312

OBJECTIVE:

A fun job with no pressure and a high salary.

3 spaces →

HIGHLIGHTS:

• Good at doing nothing
• Enjoy luxury
• Have a nice smile

WORK EXPERIENCE:

1986-88 Beach Bum, Florida

1 inch →

CALLING ATTENTION TO IMPORTANT INFORMATION

Accessories make the outfit; cosmetics make the face. In the same way, finishing flourishes transform Plain-Jane resumes into knockouts.

To make your most stunning credentials leap off the page, selectively apply these effects:

- Bullets
- Bold type
- Uppercase letters
- Underlining
- Italics
- Indenting

You should definitely accent:

- **Your name**
- **Your job titles** (if impressive and relevant to your goals)
- **Names of companies you worked for** (if impressive)
- **Name of the school you attended**
- **Impressive accomplishments**

The example below shows two versions of the same resume, one with highlighting, the other *au naturel*. You'll see the difference.

RESUME WITH HIGHLIGHTING

JOHN SMITH
16 Weatherby Road
Aspen, Colorado 21121   (303) 273-4312

OBJECTIVE:

A management position in marketing using my M.B.A. and my experience.

EXPERIENCE:

1987-89   *Ice Cream-Emporium, Paris*
                 PRODUCT MANAGER

                 Oversaw product line of 28 flavors. Managed $28m budget.
                 * Rated Best Manager, 1988.

1981-86   *Pelle Software, East Coast*
                 MARKETING DIRECTOR

                 Developed campaign for DESK software package.
                 * Promoted seven times in five years.

RESUME AU NATURAL

JOHN SMITH
16 Weatherby Road
Aspen, Colorado 21121   (303) 273-4312

OBJECTIVE:

A management position in marketing using my M.B.A. and my experience.

Experience:

1987-89   Ice-Cream Emporium, Paris
                 Product Manager

                 Oversaw product line of 28 flavors. Managed $28m budget. Rated Best Manager of 1988.

1981-86   Pelle Software, East Coast
                 Marketing Director

                 Developed campaign for DESK software package. Promoted seven times in 5 years.

FINISHING FLOURISHES

To really pack a punch, type your cover letter on letterhead that matches your resume. It's easy to make letterhead. Just type your resume heading onto a blank sheet of paper. Use the same typestyle and layout as you used for your resume. Now make copies on high quality paper. Voila! Letterhead in a flash.

You can get matching envelopes for pennies. Ask at the print shop when you order your paper.

CHAPTER 15

SPECIAL PROBLEMS

"Don't worry about your checkered past, William. I'm sure someone will want you."

"What after all is a halo? It's only one more thing to keep clean."

—Christopher Fry

"Hi Ho, Hi Ho, it's off to work we go . . ." Do you look forward to your daily stint at the mines with great delight, just like the seven dwarfs? Does your work history read like a waltz, gracefully dipping from one happy position to another? Or do you have dank corners and empty spaces in your past; a work history from hell?

If you're a job-hopper, career changer, reentering housewife, recent graduate, or have an otherwise jazzy history—stop sulking about your pockmarked past. You aren't doomed. With a little adroit maneuvering, you can accentuate your strengths, downplay your difficulties, and present a walloping good image.

"AFTER I'M A CEO, I THINK I'LL BE A PLUMBER": ADVICE FOR CAREER CHANGERS

"Do you have trouble making up your mind? Well—yes and no."

—Herbert V. Prochnow

If you spent the last 10 years selling lawn mowers and now you want to dance with the Bolshoi, you have a problem—unless you wore toe-shoes on the job. To get work in a new field, you need to show *some* relevant training or experience. That's the bad news. The good news? Even the tiniest morsel of relevant background can look grand if you know how to exploit it.

Melvin Dumstorm has been a computer programmer for 15 years. Now he wants a job as a chef. His mother and father and dog all think he's a great cook, but he never held an actual cooking job. He won't find employment simply by bragging about his yummy beef stew in a cover letter. He needs to dredge up something more substantial.

Lucky Melvin has two assets: he took cooking courses and got a certificate in Stew Cuisine, and he cooks for all family functions. How did he doctor his resume to promenade these things?

First, his Spotlight section broadcasts his kitchen skills. He lists the equipment he knows, the types of food he can prepare, the recipes he's developed.

What do you think comes after his Spotlight section? His Education section, of course. Melvin advertises his success in culinary school in bold letters, making a big deal out of his recent certificate and good grades. He also notes that his teacher was Chef Pierre Gastronique, a famous figure in stew circles.

Finally, the dread Work History section. Does Melvin merely grimace and tell about his computer work? No. He begins with this listing:

CHEF (1987–Present)
Dumstorm Kitchens, Stewville, Maine
Planned menus, oversaw food buying, managed all food preparation for numerous special events, and catered affairs for up to 100 people.

Smart Melvin capitalizes on his informal experience at home, without lying or cheating. Since he used so much space on top of his resume developing his Spotlight and Education sections, he doesn't have to worry about looking too computerish, even though the rest of his Work History includes only computer jobs.

The moral of this story: bulk up your Spotlight section to support your new goals. Don't worry about how huge your spotlight gets; you need a big flag. Play up your relevant courses, certificates, and other training. If your educational credentials outshine your work experience, put your Education section before your Work History section. And if you have *any* relevant experience—including volunteer work, internships, or informal training—list that experience right in your Work History section like any other job. If you want, you can note that the job was an internship or volunteer position in parentheses, like this:

SAILING INSTRUCTOR (internship)
Meek Marina, Fairsail, Georgia

"MY LAST 40 JOBS WEREN'T SO BAD": ADVICE FOR JOB HOPPERS

"Take this job and shove it . . ." begins a popular country-western tune. You know the song; it's your special anthem. Time and again, after two years or two months or even two minutes on the job, boredom descends and you hit the road. You're a Don Juan in the work world—no job can hold you. How can you possibly convince prospective employers that you're ready to be a stable citizen?

Assume you have a work history like Babs Tulosi, a virtuoso job hopper:

10/91 to Present:	*Dog Behaviorist,* Chow Wow Canine Center
5/91 to 9/91:	*Canine Manicurist,* Woofie World
3/91 to 5/91:	*Beautician,* Angel Face Salon
10/90 to 2/91	*Manager,* Flat Tap Corp.
9/89 to 7/90	*Behavioral Psychologist,* The Edge Counseling
6/89 to 8/89	*Colorist,* Shi Shi, Inc.
2/89 to 5/89	*Bum*
9/86 to 1/89	*Life Planning Counselor,* Karma Counseling

Should you dutifully list all of your jobs in order, like Babs did? What else *can* you do?

Babs smartened up. After receiving numerous rejections, her dream job became available—Head of the Lap-Dog Behavior Institute. She rewrote her work history, like this:

Dog Behaviorist, Chow Wow Canine Center (1991 to Present)
Behavioral Psychologist, The Edge Counseling (1989 to 1990)
Life Planning Counselor, Karma Counseling (1986 to 1989)

Does her revised history show any gaps? No. She shows a consistent work history for every year since 1986. Is it dishonest? No. She doesn't lie about dates or invent jobs. Is it effective? You bet. Babs got the job she wanted and then got bumped upstairs to the International Lap-Dog Psychoanalytic Institute, a position she loves and might actually keep.

If you've been around the universe in *your* work life, cite only your most relevant jobs and exclude the fluff. List employment by year only, just like Babs. If you really want to mention some of your short-term positions, you can append an entry like this:

Additional part-time and temporary work experience as a beautician. Worked with Shi Shi, Inc., the Angel Face Salon, and Woofie World.

Finally, remember that although you lack stability, you do offer a vast wealth of experience. Every job you have enriches you in some way. So, use your Spotlight section to show off how enriched you are. Emphasize skills and accomplishments that support your goals of the moment.

PUT THOSE KIDS IN STORAGE: ADVICE FOR REENTERING HOUSEWIVES

You raised four bratty kids, scrubbed zillions of dishes, and the world says you haven't worked for 15 years. How can you fill in the big resume gap? Should you make up some fancy name for housewife, like *"Household Engineer,"* or *"Domestic Coordinator"*? Should you invent equally fancy job responsibilities, like "coordinated travel arrangements," and "managed all finances"?

Fancying up the facts is one option. Here's another: Follow the above instructions for career changers. Put a big Skills section at the top of your resume. List your volunteer activities as regular jobs. Play up any special courses or training you received.

If you truly haven't done anything but domestic work for a very long time, you might consider taking courses, completing an internship, or doing volunteer work just to get experience. In any case, learn to network and make good use of your contacts, because your resume can only inflate the facts so much. You don't want to cross the line into deceit-land. (See the next chapter for information on networking.)

ADVICE FOR OTHERS WITH LONG HISTORIES OF UNEMPLOYMENT

Barnaby Snorkwhiz lived in a grass hut on the beach for three years, eating seaweed and fish and happily avoiding work. One day, he got sick of kelp and mud and decided to upgrade to a condo. He looked for a job, with no success. Nobody wanted to hire a career bum. How could he better represent his three years of leisure?

If, like Barnaby, you have embarrassingly long stretches of unemployment, you should follow the advice for career changers and reentering housewives. Play up volunteer experience and informal experience. Capitalize on special training. Include a bulky Skills section. Use your contacts.

If you've done absolutely *nothing* for the past several years, try to get some volunteer or internship experience. Although it may be painful to give away your time for free, even a few months of experience can increase your prospects significantly.

"I HAD A STRAIGHT-A AVERAGE SO GIVE ME A JOB": ADVICE FOR RECENT GRADUATES

"I've had seven years experience in the last three years alone."

Your degree sure looks pretty all framed and hanging over your desk, but employers don't seem moved. Everyone in the world has more experience than you. Your $100,000 degree amounts to zero because suave hot-shots with a real work history keep snatching jobs away from you.

Should you go to the Registrar's Office and demand your $100,000 back? What other options do you have?

No resume problem presents more difficulty than a complete lack of work experience. Like a reentering housewife, you need to make good use of personal contacts if you just graduated. You also need to accumulate every bit of experience you can. Try to get internships or do volunteer work until you get real work. Write up your informal or volunteer experience like a regular job in the Work History section. Even the tiniest bit of experience makes a big difference.

Build up your Spotlight section, listing all the relevant skills you have. Put your Education section right under the Spotlight. List your relevant courses, achievements, and activities, as described in Chapter 10.

What about your hamburger flipping and babysitting jobs? If you have no other work experience, go ahead and include them. You want employers to know you have held jobs before. But try to make your Education section and Spotlight sections take up more room than your descriptions of menial labor-type work.

"WAKE ME UP IN 20 YEARS": ADVICE FOR WORKERS WITH TOO MANY YEARS IN THE SAME JOB

You survived two decades at General Broom, and then were laid off. Now you need to convince employers that you can do more than push broom handles.

Years ago, workers married jobs for life. Nobody snickered at Maxwell Jones for spending his entire career with the same company. Now, employers consider Maxwell a corpse. They believe that dynamic workers try to get ahead, and therefore change jobs every three to seven years (but not more often than that).

So what can you do? First, show that staying in one place didn't hamper your acquaintance with new developments in your field. In your Spotlight section, point out the current technologies, procedures, and materials you know. Then, in your Work History section, break your entry into the jobs you held within the company or into accomplishment areas, as in these examples:

GENERAL BROOM, Sweeps, Nevada

VICE PRESIDENT OF HANDLE MARKETING (1986–91)
Oversaw budget of $3 million. Developed innovative advertising campaign that increased profits by 73 percent. Supervised staff of 53.

Accomplishments:
- Reversed company losses within one month.
- Spearheaded absorption of two subsidiary companies.
- Reduced turnover by 47 percent.

MANAGER, HANDLE DEPARTMENT (1981–85)
Developed successful training programs for staff of 100. Introduced product innovations. Developed new accounts.

Accomplishments:
- Named Manager of the Year for three consecutive years.
- New handle design increased sales by 30 percent.
- Training programs used as model by other departments.

HANDLE SALES COORDINATOR (1975–81)
Supervised sales staff of 25. Provided sales training. Wrote monthly reports.

Accomplishments:
- Promoted to this position within seven months.
- Exceeded quotas every year.

OR

GENERAL BROOM, Sweeps, Nevada

STAFF SUPERVISION AND TRAINING
- Implemented new training program adopted by all departments.
- Directly supervised up to 100 managers and sales staff.
- Completed performance evaluations on 37 staff annually.
- Reviewed all promotion decisions and firing decisions.

MARKETING
- Developed new ad campaign that increased profits 73 percent.
- Awarded "Jint Prize" for innovative ads.
- Built relationships with national media sources.
- Introduced automated systems in Marketing Department.

ADMINISTRATION
Managed annual budget of $3 million.
* Reversed company losses within one month.
* Spearheaded absorption of two subsidiary companies.
* Reduced turnover by 47 percent.

Professional History:
Vice President of Handle Marketing (1986–91)
Manager, Handle Department (1981–85)
Handle Sales Coordinator (1975–81)

"BUT I'M NOT OLD ENOUGH TO BE 'SIR' OR 'MADAM'": ADVICE FOR OLDER WORKERS

> *"You are only young once, but you can stay immature indefinitely."*
>
> —Anon.

If you number among the wrinkle generation, which these days means anything older than 40, don't advertise the fact. It's unfair and it's illegal, but employers still discriminate against older workers.

Once you waltz into the interview, you can charm employers into disregarding your birthdate. But to get to the interview stage, you'd better follow these rules:

1. Don't list jobs you held more than 20 years ago.
2. Don't list graduation dates stretching back more than 20 years.
3. Don't list memberships in senior organizations, unless you're applying for a job with a senior organization.

PART 3

BEYOND RESUMES

CHAPTER 16

MARKETING YOUR RESUME EFFECTIVELY

You finished writing your resume and can't believe how ravishing it looks? Congratulations! Enjoy your victory, but don't recline on your laurels. You still have work to do.

Once you finish composing your resume, you have to get it into the employer's face. This won't be easy, because employers prefer to occupy their faces with things like reading stockmarket pages and making pie charts. How can you get employers' attention? Should you mail out a thousand copies of your resume, all addressed to "Dear Sir"? Should you bring it to employment agencies and let them do the work? Or ask Daddy to show it to his friends downtown?

Statistics show that the Daddy method usually yields the best results. Of course, not everyone has a Daddy, and not all Daddies have friends downtown. If you have no relatives you can hit up for help, don't worry. You can still use that wonderfully hip and effective process—networking.

HOW TO NETWORK INTO THE LAP OF EMPLOYMENT

"Beat your gong and sell your candies."

—Chinese proverb

Who would you choose for a blind date: the person your best friend describes as "gorgeous, brilliant, and just like you," or the anonymous person who sticks a personal ad in the paper? You'd pick your best friend's candidate of course, even if your best friend has abysmal taste. Why? Because you trust your friend more than you trust the personals. The person in the paper could turn out to be a complete wacko or pervert.

Employers also choose people they already know—or at least know of. They fear that weirdos and lazy bums lurk behind anonymous resumes. Why should they take chances on strangers?

Of course, you're not a wacko or weirdo, but the employer doesn't know that. How can you overcome your anonymity? How can you gain credibility? Easy. Try to personally meet employers *before* you send your resume. At the least, have contacts personally recommend you to employers they know.

"I can't just go barging in on employers to introduce myself," you say. "I have no contacts who will refer me to anyone good. Anyway, I'd rather just apply to ads in the paper."

You can stick to the help-wanted ads if you want, but *networking* will most likely yield a better job, faster. Networking means making contacts, then using those contacts to make other contacts, until you finally meet someone who offers you a job.

Networkers go incognito. They don't declare that they want a job. Instead, they try to collect information about their chosen field and about particular companies from each person they talk to. Suppose someone calls you and says, "I want a job cooking breakfast. Can I cook yours?" You feel put off, say "No," and the conversation ends. Now suppose that same person calls and says, "I'm studying breakfast habits of lovable people. Can I talk to you about your breakfast for just 10 minutes, at your convenience?" Of course you'd say "Yes." You want to share your wisdom and insight.

That's how networking operates. You convince people to share their wisdom and personal experiences with you. That makes them feel good. They remember you fondly. When they hear of a good job three months later, they think of you.

Roger Reel wants to enter the field of film editing, but has no contacts. What does he do? He tells everyone he knows about his aspirations. Finally, he tells a neighbor, who happens to have a brother-in-law on the accounting staff at Warner Brothers. Roger makes an appointment to meet the brother-in-law, and gets five names from him. He meets all five people, and gets even more names. He keeps getting names and meeting people, asking things like:

- Would you recommend this work to someone like me? Why?
- What additional training do I need to get?
- What do you do in a typical day?
- What companies have the best reputation? What about your company?
- Do you know anyone else I can talk to?

Roger limits his interviews to a half hour, and gives resumes only if asked for them. He follows up every interview with a thank-you letter. Within three months, he knows exactly what type of film editing he wants to do, and even knows where he wants to do it. He now has so many contacts in his choice company that when a job opens up, he gets first consideration.

To launch your networking campaign, canvass everyone you know for names of people who might help you. You can also get names by calling relevant departments at your local colleges, by contacting local companies, and by joining professional organizations in your chosen field.

How do you set up a networking appointment? Say something like this:

"Hi. My name is Devlin Dip. I got your name from Dr. Benson Hurst. I'm an audiologist, but I've been thinking about moving into counseling work. Dr. Hurst said that you have a broad background in both audiology and clinical counseling, and that you'd be a great person for me to talk to. I wonder if you might have a half hour available to talk with me. I'm real flexible about scheduling. I can meet you anytime at your convenience within the next month or two."

USUAL AND UNUSUAL SOURCES OF JOBS

Newspaper Ads

"Here's one. 'Horseback riding instructor wanted. No experience necessary.'"

Most job seekers worship the help-wanted ads. They believe that somewhere in that tangle of fine print, the perfect job lurks, waiting to be grabbed. Every new paper brings hope and possibility. So what if 75percent of all employers never advertise in the newspaper? Why worry about the 100 other applicants who respond to every ad? Job seekers still consider the newspaper their Number One favorite tool. Why? Because it lets them look for work without ever leaving the couch.

Job seekers don't want to get involved in the ugly business of hustling to find work. Perusing the help wanteds offers an easy, dignified alternative. Unfortunately, other job hunting methods yield much better results.

Should you get off your couch and forget the help wanteds? Not entirely. When job hunting, you should use every possible method. Many people *do* find work through classified ads, and if you use a little savvy, you might too. Just promise yourself that you'll try other methods as well.

To get a response from a help-wanted ad, always call before sending in your resume. Ask some astute questions about the position ("What type of person are you looking for?"; "Can you tell me more about the responsibilities?"; "Can you send me information about your organization?"). Calling ahead lets you gather information you can use to customize your cover letter. Also, if you sound intelligent, the employer might ask for your name and then watch for your resume.

If you can't call ahead, at least include a customized cover letter. NEVER SEND A RESUME WITHOUT A COVER LETTER. Tailor the letter to the advertised position. If the ad asks for someone with five years of editing experience and a sense of humor, talk about your extensive editing background and your great sense of humor. (For more information on cover letters, see page 95.)

Internal Postings

Many companies, schools, hospitals, and other employers post job openings on company bulletin boards and newsletters instead of advertising them to the public. Find out if the companies that interest you have internal postings. If so, visit those companies frequently to stay informed about new jobs.

Professional Organizations

Find out if professional organizations in your field maintain a job bank, publish newletters or journals that list job openings, or sponsor professional conferences where you could meet potential employers.

Agencies of All Stripes

If you use employment agencies, choose those that specialize in your line of work. They'll have the best contacts in your field, and won't send you to interviews outside your area of interest or level of competence. To find a reputable agency, watch the help wanteds. Some agencies list the same ad week after week. They don't have real job openings. They just want to build a backlog of candidates in case a real job opens up. Try to get referrals to good agencies from people you know.

To get results from your agent, call frequently. Most agents see scores of new candidates each week. They work on a resume for a few days, then move on to new ones. To make sure your agent remembers you, keep calling.

Should you pay a placement fee? Absolutely not. Reputable agencies charge fees to employers, not to job candidates.

The "Shotgun Approach"

This is when you mass-mail your resumes to lots of companies, whether or not they have advertised openings. Mass mailers usually address their resumes to the Personnel Department. This method breeds heartbreak and failure. Personnel offices specialize in screening out resumes. They check incoming resumes against a rigid code of qualifications that might not fit your background. You'll get eliminated even if you have talents that more than compensate for your shortcomings.

So NEVER send your resume to Personnel if you can help it. Always try to get the name of the person who will make the ultimate hiring decision. Send your resume directly to that person. Why give personnel a chance to reject you? Go directly to the top. And always try to make personal contact with the employer first. To employers, an unsolicited resume in the mail is just another unwanted advertisement headed for the trash.

Other Avenues

- *College Placement Offices.* Most colleges offer placement services for students and alumni.
- *State and Federal Employment Offices.* Offer job listings to any member of the public, for free.
- *The Yellow Pages, the Chamber of Commerce, Corporate Directories.* Check these sources for lists of companies to approach.

COVER LETTERS

You're beautiful, you're in great shape, and the sun is shining. Do you take off your bathing suit at the beach? Not unless you want to spend the night in jail. Propriety demands that you cover up your beautiful flesh. Likewise, your beautiful resume requires a nice wrap. Sending a naked resume is as gauche as disrobing at the shore.

Employers do not ignore your cover letters in their great haste to get to your resume—many employers take cover letters very seriously. They examine your cover letter to see if you can write coherent English and to get a sense of your personal style. Also, they look for clues about things not mentioned in your resume.

Naturally, you want your cover letter to entice readers. Form cover letters ("Enclosed please find . . .") simply won't do. Your cover letters need to grab attention and speak directly to the employer's deepest needs. How? You must personalize every cover letter you write. Follow these rules:

- Always address your cover letter to a specific person. If you meet or talk to that person first, you can start your letter with a warm opening, like "Thank you so much for talking with me yesterday about . . ."
- If you answer an ad that doesn't give a person's name, call the company and ask who to send your resume to. If you absolutely can't get a name, address the letter "To Whom It May Concern." Never address a letter to "Sirs," or "Gentlemen." The woman in charge of hiring won't appreciate it.
- State the reasons why the company or position interests you. If you don't know, at least state that you're very interested in the position.
- Always respond directly to the employer's requirements. If the employer wants "background in tea brewing," talk about your tea expertise. If the employer wants someone "who can work under pressure," tell how well you do under pressure. When you call employers, ask for details about what qualifications they seek, then respond point by point to their needs. If you don't have all the qualifications the employer wants, don't point out what you lack. Instead, capitalize on those qualifications you *do* have.
- Be concise. One page is plenty.
- Don't crowd the page. Use bullets.
- Use good quality paper. It makes a difference.
- Never handwrite cover letters. Type or print them on a letter-quality printer.

The sample cover letters on the next pages are real-life examples that successfully won interviews and, in the case of the first two letters, led to job offers.

SAMPLE COVER LETTER 1

Dear Mark:

Thanks for speaking to me on the phone yesterday about the position of Regional Bakery Supervisor. I really appreciate your taking the time to talk to me about this extremely interesting position. As you suggested, I have enclosed my resume for your review.

As I mentioned in our conversation, I currently supervise production at the Johnson House Grill, a busy restaurant and catering company with three locations and an annual gross of nearly $2 million. I have very strong organizational, leadership, and production skills. My experience includes:

- Supervising production and maintaining standards in the operation's three locations
- Supervising a staff of 20, including training, hiring, and firing
- Purchasing and overseeing maintenance of equipment and services
- Buying bakery and restaurant ingredients

- Controlling distribution and commissary operations
- Food costing; inventory, cost, and quality control
- Product development
- Overseeing catering production

Prior to my current position, I opened a small restaurant in San Francisco. I was involved in all phases including designing, building and finishing the space, purchasing and installing equipment, developing and producing the product line, staffing, and advertising. Therefore, I have first-hand experience with the difficulties and challenges of getting a new operation off the ground on schedule and according to standards.

I am familiar with a wide variety of bakery (and restaurant) equipment. Specifically, I have used Hobart mixers of all sizes (including grating and slicing attachments), Garland dry deck ovens, convection ovens, five-shelf rotary ovens, pizza ovens, slicers, bread slicers, electric and gas proof boxes, burr mixers, sheeters, buffalo choppers, and gas steam kettles.

During our conversation, you also mentioned that you were looking for someone capable of grasping and implementing your system without having to reinvent all of the research and experience that it took to develop it. I believe that one of my greatest strengths is the ability to quickly understand operating systems and to put their principles into action.

Thank you again for introducing me to Arnoff. I would be very interested in meeting with you to provide further information and to discuss ways in which we might work together. I look forward to hearing from you.

Sincerely,

SAMPLE COVER LETTER 2

Dear Ms. Rose:

I am responding to your recent advertisement for a Technical Editor. My background includes:

- Experience editing technical materials for a wide range of companies including Microsoft, Inc., Wang, and Apple.
- Experience as the sole editor for the systems documentation group at Digital Equipment Corporation in Philadelphia.
- Substantial experience providing developmental editing, copyediting, and rewriting of specification guidelines, reference manuals, and on-line help screens.
- Extensive project management experience.
- Familiarity with a broad range of software and hardware, including IBM, Macintosh, and Digital systems.

In addition to the above experience, I instruct a course in Technical Editing Skills at Dearborn Community College. I'm a fast and precise editor, and enjoy juggling numerous projects at once.

I'm impressed with everything I've heard about Desktop Systems, and I certainly enjoy using your software. I'd love to contribute my expertise to your company, and look forward to hearing from you.

Thanks for your consideration.

Sincerely,

SAMPLE COVER LETTER 3

Dear Mr. Marks:

Thank you for taking the time to speak to me on the phone today about the position of Instructor of Sociology. Our conversation heightened my interest in the position and I have enclosed my resume for your review.

I have extensive teaching experience in collaborative and nontraditional settings. At both the University of Chicago and the Berkeley College of Music, I was a member of teams that developed and taught courses aimed at stimulating critical thinking, developing writing skills, and introducing students to issues in sociology, psychology, economics, philosophy, and a broad range of subjects in the liberal arts.

At the University of Chicago, I was a member of the remedial writing component of the Freshman English program. As a Liberal Arts Instructor at Berkeley, I co-developed and taught Freshman English, including a remedial writing component. In both cases, I worked with students who had difficulties with language and who came to higher education from a wide variety of paths. Many of the students were adult learners.

My strengths as a teacher include patience, humor, the ability to render complex ideas in simple language, imagination, and the ability to identify and engage the strengths of the students. I am open to and interested in a variety of approaches to teaching.

Currently, I'm the Director of Basic Skills, Inc., a literacy program for low-income adults. My accomplishments include increasing the funding base by 50 percent and adding five satellite offices to the program.

I have read about Delvine College in the past and would be very interested in being a part of its worthy program.

If you need additional information, or if you want to contact me for an interview, please call me at (717) 635-7091. Thank you very much for your consideration.

Sincerely,

SAMPLE COVER LETTER 4

Dear Ms. Hamilton:

Thank you so much for sending me literature on Rencine Corporation. I certainly was impressed with the material, particularly with the descriptions of the company's corporate climate and long-range marketing goals.

As I mentioned in our conversation, I was the Vice-President/Merchandise Manager of The Clothes Horse in Manhasset, New York from 1974 to 1979. In that time, I achieved a 16 percent pre-tax profit, successfully redirected the product line from high fashion to basics, and improved annual sales from $1 million to $14 million.

After leaving The Clothes Horse, I became President/CEO of The Gap, Inc. My accomplishments in that position include:

- Moving the company from an annual loss situation to profitability within one year.
- Diversifying the product line from 100 percent Levis to over 60 different product lines.
- Increasing inventory turns from 2× to 5× within three years.

I'm looking for a new challenge at the current time, and would be most interested in using my skills and expertise in a dynamic corporation such as yours. I'll be in Chicago the last two weeks of May, and if your schedule allows, I'd appreciate an opportunity to meet with you at that time to discuss how my background might suit your needs. I'll call you in a week to see if we can arrange something.

In the meantime, you can reach me at (518) 490-7412. I look forward to speaking with you again.

Sincerely,

MORE FOOT-IN-THE-DOOR TACTICS

Unconventional Delivery

If you receive 10 regular-looking pieces of mail and one Federal Express package, which do you open first? That mysterious Federal Express package, of course. Employers are bombarded with boring, regular mail every day. So if you have a strong interest in a particular job, splurge and send your resume by Overnight Mail. Employers will immediately assume that your interest in the position far exceeds that of other candidates. They'll also assume that you have good qualities such as determination and ingenuity. The fact is, although your resume must follow conventional format, your method of delivery doesn't need to.

Some candidates score big by delivering their resumes in person. You need patience and chutzpah to use this method, but if you feel brave, give it a try. When you arrive at the office, don't just hand your resume to the receptionist: try to see the person in charge of hiring. Find out the name of the employer by calling ahead of time, and ask for that person by name.

If the employer isn't available when you arrive, offer to wait. Say that you have a few questions about the job, and that you need just a few minutes. You can also try setting up an appointment for a more convenient time. When you finally see the employer, apologize for barging in, ask a few good questions, stay only several minutes, and follow up with a thank-you note.

What about truly exotic approaches, like wearing a sandwich-board advertising your availability, or dropping resumes from a helicopter? People *have* gotten jobs using such methods, but more dignified alternatives usually yield better results, plus save your reputation.

Gracious Gratitude

Everyone likes getting personal notes in the mail. Give employers a thrill by sending personal thank-you notes at every opportunity. If employers meet you for an informational interview, send a nice thank-you note immediately after. If employers help you on the telephone, send a nice note of thanks. Every piece of mail you send plugs your name one more time. Plus, you can use the thank-you letter to remind employers of your special qualifications.

You certainly should send a thank-you note after interviewing for an actual job. Even if you get rejected, send a follow-up note expressing your continued interest in the company. You never know what the future will bring.

If you think an employer will appreciate something offbeat, try sending your thanks by telegram. You'll certainly make an impression.

Here's a sample thank-you letter:

Dear Ms. Fin:

I enjoyed meeting you yesterday, and want to thank you for your thorough description of the position available with Sudsy Scuba Tours. I was particularly interested to learn that Sudsy will be starting a new program in Cozumel, and that if offered the position, I would be Dive Director. As I mentioned to you in the interview, I spent five years underwater in Cozumel (1983–87) during my dive training with Snorkel-Face, Inc. I believe my familiarity with the fish and reefs in that area would be of great benefit. I am also excited by the possibility of using my background in public relations to promote the Cozumel program.

From what you told me, and from my own observation, I believe Sudsy offers exactly what I am looking for. I realize that considerable hard work would be required to launch the Cozumel program. I would undertake that work with the energy and enthusiasm the program deserves.

Sincerely,

CHAPTER 17

INTERVIEW FINESSE

NOTHING BEATS INTERVIEWING FOR GETTING YOUR MIND OFF THE SOAPS

Imagine spending your days traveling to new places, wearing elegant clothes, dining out, and meeting powerful people who listen attentively to your every word. That's the interviewing life.

You wouldn't describe interviewing in such glowing terms? To you, interviewing means answering nosy questions, sweating up your clothes, and then getting rejected by a pompous nerd who can't even pronounce your name?

If you fear and loathe the interview process, you need to change your attitude. Why? Because people who enjoy interviewing get many more job offers than people who don't. It's a secret law of the Universe: the Law of Magnetic Attraction. People who love interviewing attract jobs.

"Boy, this book is really degenerating," you think, "sliding into mystical hogwash." Oh yeah? Think about this.

Lester Turmoil hates interviewing. In fact, he hates the whole job hunt process. With great effort, he sends out 90 resumes, then sits by the telephone hoping for a miracle. A miracle happens: Lester gets called for an interview. He slinks into the employer's office, offers a sweaty palm, nervously answers questions, and hopes the interrogation ends soon. He forgets the questions he wanted to ask, spills coffee on the rug, and wears a funeral face throughout. When he returns home, he sits by the phone waiting for another miracle, but this time God is less kind. Lester blew it.

Mary Sunstein, on the other hand, approaches interviews with gusto. She looks forward to meeting new employers and finding out about new companies. "You learn something new in every interview," she says. Mary projects genuine interest and a positive attitude to employers; she radiates enthusiasm, interest, and confidence. She gets offered Lester's job, and several others as well.

THE RIGHT ATTITUDE MEANS EVERYTHING (ALMOST)

Job seekers often make one big mistake. They assume that employers care mostly about credentials and competence. More than anything, employers want enthusiastic, willing, grateful employees who learn quickly, don't complain, don't give lip, and don't need mental health counseling every two minutes.

If employers cared only for credentials, why would they give interviews? They could pick candidates based on resumes alone. Employers interview you for two reasons: to see if you would be a fun person to boss around, and to determine if you have enough dynamism to get the job done. Remember—by the time employers call you in, they've already seen your resume and have determined that you possess the requisite credentials. The interview isn't about credentials. It's about personality.

You don't want anyone assessing your verve? And you don't find it so easy to muster verve, anyway? These pointers will help you:

HOW TO ENJOY YOUR INTERVIEW:

☐ 1. Consider that the interview serves *two* people, both you and the employer. Don't you want to know what you'll be getting into if you take the job? Don't you want to know if you can tolerate the employer? If the job will kill you? The interview gives you an opportunity to uncover the sorry (or happy) truth about the position. So stop worrying about the impression you make and start thinking of the interview as an important research expedition.

☐ 2. Realize that the interviewer may be even more nervous than you. Many employers conduct interviews infrequently and feel very uncomfortable with the process.

☐ 3. Recognize that employers need you as much as you need them. Employers interview you when they have so much work to do that they can't even find the time to read "Peanuts." They *want* to read "Peanuts"; they need your help. Because they feel desperate, they *want* you to be the right candidate. They can't afford to waste thousands of hours interviewing poor prospects.

☐ 4. View the interview as a rare opportunity to talk unabashedly about yourself to a captive audience.

☐ 5. If you still can't muster any enthusiasm, think about the silver hope each interview holds. You just may find the fat paycheck, indulgent boss, long vacations, and fun-filled work of your dreams.

FANCY INTERVIEW DUDS

"One obvious way to remain calm and perspiration free during an interview, of course, is narcotics, but there you run into the problem of scratching yourself and trying to steal things off the interviewer's desk. So as a precaution, what most veteran employment counselors recommend is that you wear 'dress shields,' which, as some of you women already know, are these highly absorbent devices that you stuff into your armpits. They are available in bulk at any good employment agency. For a job interview, you should stuff three or four shields into each pit."

—Dave Barry, *Claw Your Way to the Top*

Does it really matter what you wear to an interview? Yes, yes, yes. Would you buy a bagel without a hole? Of course not. A bagel should look bagel-like. In the same way, employers expect you to look worker-like. What do workers look like? Like funeral attendees. Workers dress in mourning clothes. Dark suits. Few accessories. Nothing flashy. The tradition got started during the Industrial Revolution when people first realized that every day at work brings you two days closer to death.

Employers have an immediate chemical reaction to you that colors their ultimate decision. Wearing the right clothing can sway chemistry in your favor. Follow these tips:

GENDER-FREE ADVICE

- [ ] No matter what type of job you interview for, you can't go wrong in a conservative suit. According to experts, dark blue and gray pinstripe make the best impression.
- [ ] It does no good to dress properly if you look unkempt and smell bad. Be sure to clean your nails and hands at least up to the sleeves, and wash your face and neck down to the collar.
- [ ] Avoid flashy jewelry and watches.
- [ ] If you must wear cologne, wear only the teeniest amount. Also, watch out for smelly soaps and after-shave. The smell you love may be the employer's nemesis.
- [ ] Don't eat garlic or onions before the interview.
- [ ] Avoid loafers, sandals, sneakers, and platform shoes.
- [ ] Don't wear political buttons. Cover your tattoos. Clean your briefcase.

SPECIALLY FOR MEN

- [ ] Wear a long-sleeved shirt.
- [ ] Nothing looks more gauche than short, white socks hanging out under your pant legs. Wear long, dark socks that cover your calves.

☐ Polish your shoes, and make sure they don't have worn-down heels.

☐ Tuck in your shirttail.

☐ Don't have pens and garbage bulging out from your shirt pocket. Don't have keys dangling from a chain on your belt. Don't wear a pen behind your ear.

☐ Get a haircut. In the interview world, long hair, spiked hair, streaked hair, and other stylish flair finds no welcome.

SPECIALLY FOR WOMEN

☐ Suits are de rigueur for women, too. Don't show up in your lovely Laura Ashley dress. Employers want workers who dress like they mean business.

☐ Don't forget to wear a slip.

☐ Wear nylons—not cotton tights or anklets. Beware of ugly runs. Bring an extra pair of stockings with you in case snags develop en route.

☐ Don't wear overly high heels. You should be able to walk comfortably.

☐ Don't wear dangly earrings, low-cut necklines, above-the-knee hemlines, or anything else that reminds the employer that you're not just "one of the guys."

☐ Pull your hair into a conservative, super-neat style, even if you look better with a frizzed-out mane.

☐ Avoid extra-long nails, bright nail polish, and too much make-up.

☐ Don't carry shopping bags with you. And clean out your pocketbook. You might need to open it in front of the interviewer.

PREPARING FOR THE INTERVIEW ADVENTURE

"Adventure is the result of poor planning."

—Colonel Blatchford Snell

You love improvisation and don't want to prepare for your interviews? Job hunting isn't theater. If you want to make a good impression, you need to prepare ahead. Follow these guidelines:

Do Background Research

Most interviewers ask why you want the job. Here's the typical answer: "I don't really know very much about the job. Can you tell me a little more?" Right from the start, most candidates show their ignorance.

You want to be a brilliant candidate? Then don't get caught with your pants down—prepare ahead of time. Find out everything you can about the company, the employer, and the job.

When employers call you for an interview, ask if they can send you a job description and company literature. Most employers will happily do so. Other good sources of information include the Chamber of Commerce and corporate directories such as *Standard & Poor*. You can also look at products the company manufactures, talk to current employees, or try to find articles in newspapers and magazines.

Informed candidates answer questions with more confidence, know more clearly what interviewers need, and prepare intelligent questions ahead of time. It sure impresses employers when it's clear that you had the foresight, thoroughness, and interest to do research on the company. And when you show that you like the company and really do want the job, employers get a special thrill.

Review Your Resume

In the excitement of the interview, you may forget important things, like your name and your ethnic origin. That's why you should review your resume before the interview.

The best way to satisfy anxious interviewers is to convince them that you performed well in similar positions before. So review your previous achievements. Think of anecdotes that show how well you handled difficult problems.

You also should prepare to discuss your special problems. The interviewer may find those blemishes in your background so cleverly buried at the bottom of your resume. You were fired? You spent three years practicing "circle dances of the sun" in Tahiti? No matter what your peculiar flaws, practice presenting them in a positive way. Emphasize how much you learned from each sad experience, how you gained new strength and insight, how your unfortunate experiences were isolated incidents in your otherwise successful work life.

POPULAR INTERVIEW QUESTIONS

Sooner or later, every interviewer will ask you questions. It helps to prepare your answers ahead of time. If possible, practice interviewing with a friend. If you have no friends, you can rent them for about $7 an hour.

Of course, you can't predict exactly what an interviewer will ask, but most interviewers ask at least some of these questions:

- Why do you want this job?
- Why do you want to leave your current job?
- Why were you out of work for so long?
- How long a commitment could you make to this job?
- What were your responsibilities in your last position?
- What did you like most in your last position? What did you like least?
- How do you handle pressure?
- Why should we hire you for this job?
- What are your strengths? What are your weaknesses?
- What are your long-range career goals? Your five-year goals?

- What type of work environment do you prefer?
- What special problems have you encountered in your work, and how have you handled them?
- What was your worst failure? Your greatest success?
- What gives you satisfaction in your work?
- What are your salary expectations?
- Do you have references I can call?
- Do you have any questions?

Tricky Questions

Why Do You Want to Leave Your Current Job? In this case, honesty doesn't pay. "Because my boss eats toads and I hate my desk," won't win any offers. More acceptable answers include, "I'm happy in my current job, but I need a new challenge," or "I'm happy in my current job, but I've heard great things about your company. The available job sounds so intriguing I just *had* to apply."

What Are Your Weaknesses? This question is a favorite among sadistic employers why love to watch candidates squirm. Don't squirm. Prepare a smart answer. The best weaknesses, from the employer's point of view, are those that show you have an over-conscientious nature. Things like, "I work too hard," "I sometimes don't know my limits," "I pay too much attention to detail," or "I need to stop doing everything for my co-workers and give others a chance to excel."

What Are Your Salary Expectations? Try to avoid answering this question in a first interview. If you must respond, turn the question around ("What range were *you* thinking of?") If that doesn't work, say "My requirements depend on the total compensation and on the responsibilities of the position. I need to think about it." Eventually, you might have to suggest a figure. It helps if you do research ahead of time. Find out what people in comparable positions in other companies make. In any case, suggest a raise 15 to 20 percent above your current salary.

Do You Have References I Can Call? Who should you give for a reference? Your spouse or mother won't do. Try to think of people from your current or previous job who will say nice things about you. It's always best to name your current boss, but if you can't, give co-workers as references. Famous or prominent people in your field, academic advisors, and bosses from old jobs also suffice.

It looks good if you have a pretyped list of three to five references with you. Include name, address, phone number, and position of each person listed.

Only use people for references if you're sure they like you. Ask them what they'll say about you. If you notice they have their fingers crossed when they answer, or you otherwise feel uncertain about their reliability, find other references. Or, you can verify the reliability of your references by asking a friend—posing as a prospective employer—to call for a reference check.

Once you've unearthed people who'll advocate you, brief them ahead of time. Tell them what jobs you're applying for and what you hope they'll say on your behalf.

What You Should Ask

Smart interviewees always have questions. Your questions show employers that you have genuine interest in the position. Unfortunately, interview etiquette prohibits asking the really important questions like "How far are you from the nearest mall?" and "How much money do *you* make?" You have to ask more subdued questions. Here are some examples:

- When would the position begin?
- How would I spend my time in a typical day?
- Who would I report to? Who would report to me? Who would I work with?
- What is the most important aspect of the position?
- Is this a new position? If not, where is the person who had the position before me?
- Can you describe the corporate climate?
- Why do you like working here?

INTERVIEW DEMEANOR

You don your blue suit and your chipper attitude, practice interviewing with three rented friends, and finally, drive off to the interview. What could possibly go wrong? Plenty. Wearing the right clothes and knowing smart answers will do no good if you curse at the interviewer, have a slimy handshake, or otherwise violate the interview code of ethics. Review these rules:

☐ **Arrive early.** Employers will resent you before the interview starts if you keep them waiting. Plus, they'll assume you'd have punctuality problems on the job.

☐ **The interview starts in the parking lot.** To make difficult decisions, employers spend lots of time staring out of windows until wisdom dawns. If they happen to be watching when you pull up, you'd better be on good behavior. Fighting over parking spots, combing your hair and putting on makeup outside the car, and dropping papers all over the street won't make a good impression.

☐ **Don't slump in the lobby.** The interviewer may sneak up and find you smoking, chewing gum, listening to your headphones, and reading *the National Enquirer*. To make a good first impression, sit up straight and read company literature.

☐ **Powder your palms.** Don't slimy handshakes nauseate you? They disgust interviewers too. Dry your hands if they're sweaty, and remember—give a firm handshake (women too).

☐ **Stand tall.** Walk briskly into the interviewer's office.

☐ **Carry money with you.** The interviewer may want to go out for coffee or lunch with you.

☐ **Look relaxed.** Don't keep your coat on throughout the interview. Don't clutch your pocketbook or briefcase on your lap. Don't crack your knuckles, twirl your hair, or do anything spastic with your hands.

☐ **Make eye contact.** Look interested. And don't stare at papers on the employer's desk.

☐ **Remember to listen attentively.** Everyone loves a good listener. If you listen carefully, you'll learn what the interviewer really wants, which will help you answer questions smartly.

☐ **Don't complain about the horrors of your past job.** No matter how much you hated your last job, don't blab about it. Interviewers will assume you have trouble adjusting and getting along with people.

☐ **Communicate.** Let your interest in the position show. Tell the interviewer verbally and by your attitude that you want the job.

FOLLOWING UP

Remember to send a thank-you note after the interview. If you don't hear from the interviewer within a week, don't hesitate to call and ask about the status of the search. Most employers won't mind; many will actually appreciate your enthusiasm.

If you don't get the job, send a letter anyway. Thank the employer again, assert your continued interest in the company, and say you hope you can work together in the future. You'll make a walloping good impression, and you just may get a call sometime down the road.

APPENDIX 1

RESUME FORMAT SHEETS

PROFESSIONAL RESUME WITH SUMMARY STATEMENT

_____
Your Name (CAPS)

_____
Your Address

_____
Your Phone Number

SUMMARY OF QUALIFICATIONS

_____
_____
_____
_____
_____
_____
_____

PROFESSIONAL EXPERIENCE:

_____ , (19___ to 19___)
Job Title (CAPS)

_____ , _____
Company Name (bold and underline)   Company Location (normal text)

Enter Job Description Below:

_____
_____
_____
_____
_____

Accomplishments:
* _____
* _____
* _____
* _____
* _____

_____ , (19___ to 19___)
Job Title (CAPS)

_____ , _____
Company Name (bold and underline)   Company Location (normal text)

Enter Job Description Below:

_____
_____
_____
_____
_____

Accomplishments:
* _____
* _____
* _____
* _____
* _____

_____ , (19___ to 19___)
Job Title (CAPS)

_____ , _____
Company Name (bold and underline)   Company Location (normal text)

Enter Job Description Below:

_____
_____
_____
_____
_____
_____

Accomplishments:
*
* _____
* _____
* _____
* _____

_____ , (19___ to 19___)
Job Title (CAPS)

_____ , _____
Company Name (bold and underline)   Company Location (normal text)

Enter Job Description Here

_____
_____
_____
_____
_____

Accomplishments:
*
* _____
* _____
* _____
* _____

_____ , (19___ to 19___)
Job Title (CAPS)

_____ , _____
Company Name (bold and underline)   Company Location (normal text)

Enter Job Description Below:

_____
_____
_____
_____
_____

Accomplishments:
*
* _____
* _____
* _____
* _____

EDUCATION

_____ ,   _____
School Name (CAPS)   School Location (normal)

_____ in _____ , 19_____
Degree (bold, underlined)   Major (bold, underlined)

(Honors, Awards, Special Accomplishments) _____
* _____
* _____

_____ ,   _____
School Name (CAPS)   School Location (normal)

_____ in _____ , 19_____
Degree (bold, underlined)   Major (bold, underlined)

(Honors, Awards, Special Accomplishments) _____
* _____
* _____

Professional Development Courses: _____
_____
_____
_____

PROFESSIONAL ORGANIZATIONS/CERTIFICATIONS/
SPECIAL SKILLS/OTHER FRILLS (choose one)

_____
_____
_____
_____
_____
_____

INTERESTS/ACTIVITITES

_____
_____
* _____
* _____
* _____

References provided upon request.

PROFESSIONAL RESUME WITH HIGHLIGHTS

_____
Your Name (CAPS)

_____
Your Street Address

_____
Your City, State, and Zip Code

_____
Your Phone Number

HIGHLIGHTS

● _____

● _____

● _____

● _____

● _____

PROFESSIONAL EXPERIENCE:

_____ , (19___ to 19___)
Job Title (CAPS)

_____ , _____
Company Name (bold and underline)   Company Location (normal text)

Enter Job Description Below:

_____
_____
_____
_____
_____

Accomplishments:
* _____
* _____
* _____
* _____
* _____

_____ , (19___ to 19___)
Job Title (CAPS)

_____ , _____
Company Name (bold and underline)   Company Location (normal text)

Enter Job Description Below:

_____
_____
_____
_____
_____

Accomplishments:
* _____
* _____
* _____
* _____
* _____

_____ , (19___ to 19___)
Job Title (CAPS)

_____ , _____
Company Name (bold and underline)   Company Location (normal text)

Enter Job Description Below:

_____
_____
_____
_____

Accomplishments:
* _____
* _____
* _____
* _____
* _____

_____ , (19___ to 19___)
Job Title (CAPS)

_____ , _____
Company Name (bold and underline)   Company Location (normal text)

Enter Job Description Below:

_____
_____
_____
_____
_____

Accomplishments:
* _____
* _____
* _____
* _____
* _____

_____ , (19___ to 19___)
Job Title (CAPS)

_____ , _____
Company Name (bold and underline)   Company Location (normal text)

Enter Job Description Below:

_____
_____
_____
_____
_____

Accomplishments:
* _____
* _____
* _____
* _____
* _____

EDUCATION

_____ ,   _____
School Name (CAPS)   School Location (normal)

_____ in _____ , 19_____
Degree (bold, underlined)   Major (bold, underlined)

(Honors, Awards, Special Accomplishments) _____
* _____
* _____

_____ ,   _____
School Name (CAPS)   School Location (normal)

_____ in _____ , 19_____
Degree (bold, underlined)   Major (bold, underlined)

(Honors, Awards, Special Accomplishments) _____
* _____
Ψ _____

Professional Development Courses: _____
_____
_____
_____

PROFESSIONAL ORGANIZATIONS/CERTIFICATIONS/
SPECIAL SKILLS/OTHER FRILLS (choose one)

_____
_____
_____
_____
_____

INTERESTS/ACTIVITITES

_____
_____
_____
* _____
* _____
* _____

References provided upon request.

PROFESSIONAL RESUME WITH SKILLS SECTION

_____
Your Name (CAPS)

_____
Your Street Address

_____
Your City, State, and Zip Code

_____
Your Phone Number

AREAS OF EXPERTISE (SKILLS)

_____
Write name of first skill category here (lowercase bold and UL)

- _____
- _____
- _____
- _____
- _____
- _____
- _____

_____
Write name of second skill category here (lowercase bold and UL)

- _____
- _____
- _____
- _____
- _____
- _____
- _____

_____
Write name of third skill category here (lowercase bold and UL)

- _____
- _____
- _____
- _____
- _____
- _____
- _____

PROFESSIONAL EXPERIENCE:

_____ , (19___ to 19___)
Job Title (CAPS)

_____ , _____
Company Name (bold and underline)   Company Location (normal text)

Enter Job Description Below:

_____
_____
_____
_____
_____

Accomplishments:

*
*_____
*_____
_____

_____ , (19___ to 19___)
Job Title (CAPS)

_____ , _____
Company Name (bold and underline)   Company Location (normal text)

Enter Job Description Below:

_____
_____
_____
_____
_____

Accomplishments:
*
*_____
*_____
_____

_____ , (19___ to 19___)
Job Title (CAPS)

_____ , _____
Company Name (bold and underline)   Company Location (normal text)

Enter Job Description Below:

_____
_____
_____
_____
_____

Accomplishments:
*
*_____
*_____
_____

_____ , (19___ to 19___)
Job Title (CAPS)

_____ , _____
Company Name (bold and underline)   Company Location (normal text)

Enter Job Description Below:

_____
_____
_____
_____
_____

Accomplishments (optional):
*
*_____
*_____

_____ , (19___ to 19___)
Job Title (CAPS)

_____ , _____
Company Name (bold and underline)   Company Location (normal text)

Enter Job Description Below:

_____
_____
_____
_____
_____

Accomplishments (optional):
*
* _____
* _____

EDUCATION

_____ , _____
School Name (CAPS)   School Location (normal)

_____ in _____ , 19_____
Degree (bold, underlined)   Major (bold, underlined)

(Honors, Awards, Special Accomplishments) _____
*
* _____
* _____

_____ , _____
School Name (CAPS)   School Location (normal)

_____ in _____ , 19_____
Degree (bold, underlined)   Major (bold, underlined)

(Honors, Awards, Special Accomplishments) _____
*
* _____
* _____

Professional Development Courses: _____
_____
_____

PROFESSIONAL ORGANIZATIONS/CERTIFICATIONS/
HONORS/OTHER FRILLS (choose one)

_____
_____
_____
_____

INTERESTS/ACTIVITITES

_____
_____
_____

References provided upon request.

TECHNICAL RESUME (For Computer Professionals)

_____
Your Name (CAPS)

_____
Your Street Address

_____
Your City, State, and Zip Code

_____
Your Phone Number

SUMMARY

_____
_____
_____

TECHNICAL EXPERTISE

Hardware

_____
_____
_____

Software

_____
_____
_____

Operating Systems

_____
_____
_____

Languages

_____
_____
_____

WORK HISTORY

_____ , (19___ to 19___)
Job Title (CAPS)

_____ , _____
Company Name (bold and underline)   Company Location (normal text)

Enter Job Description Below:

_____
_____
_____
_____
_____
_____

Accomplishments:

- _____
- _____
- _____
- _____
- _____

_____ , (19___ to 19___)
Job Title (CAPS)

_____ ,_____
Company Name (bold and underline)   Company Location (normal text)

Enter Job Description Below:

_____
_____
_____
_____
_____
_____
_____

Accomplishments:

● _____
● _____
● _____
● _____
● _____

_____ , (19___ to 19___)
Job Title (CAPS)

_____ ,_____
Company Name (bold and underline)   Company Location (normal text)

Enter Job Description Below:

_____
_____
_____
_____
_____
_____
_____

Accomplishments:

● _____
● _____
● _____
● _____
● _____

_____ , (19___ to 19___)
Job Title (CAPS)

_____ ,_____
Company Name (bold and underline)   Company Location (normal text)

Enter Job Description Below:

_____
_____
_____
_____
_____
_____

Accomplishments:

● _____
● _____
● _____
● _____
● _____

_____ , (19___ to 19___)

Job Title (CAPS)

_____ , _____

Company Name (bold and underline)   Company Location (normal text)

Enter Job Description Below:

_____

_____

_____

_____

_____

_____

Accomplishments:

- _____
- _____
- _____
- _____
- _____

EDUCATION

_____ , _____

School Name (CAPS)   School Location (normal)

_____ in _____ , 19____

Degree (bold, underlined)   Major (bold, underlined)

* _____

(Honors, Awards, Special Accomplishments)

* _____

* _____

_____ , _____

School Name (CAPS)   School Location (normal)

_____ in _____ , 19____

Degree (bold, underlined)   Major (bold, underlined)

* _____

(Honors, Awards, Special Accomplishments)

* _____

* _____

ADDITIONAL COURSES: _____

_____

_____

_____

PROFESSIONAL ORGANIZATIONS/ HONORS/OTHER FRILLS (Choose one)

_____

_____

_____

_____

_____

INTERESTS/ ACTIVITIES

_____

_____

_____

_____

_____

REFERENCES   Provided upon request.

CONSULTANT/FREELANCER RESUME

_____
Your Name (CAPS)

_____
Your Street Address

_____
Your City, State, and Zip Code

_____
Your Phone Number

HIGHLIGHTS

- _____
  _____
- _____
  _____
- _____
  _____
- _____
  _____
- _____
  _____

PROFESSIONAL EXPERIENCE:

_____ , (19___ to 19___)
Job Title (CAPS)

_____ , _____
Company Name (bold and underline)   Company Location (normal text)

Enter Short Job Description Below :

_____
_____
_____

Major clients include:

_____ , _____ :
Client Name (CAP and bold and UL)   Location (normal text)

Enter short description of project below:

_____
_____
_____

_____ , _____ :
Client Name (CAP and bold and UL)   Location (normal text)

Enter short description of project below:

_____
_____

_____ , _____ :
Client Name (CAP and bold and UL)   Location (normal text)

Enter short description of project below:

_____

_____

_____

_____ , _____ :
Client Name (CAP and bold and UL)   Location (normal text)

Enter short description of project below:

_____

_____

_____

_____ , _____ :
Client Name (CAP and bold and UL)   Location (normal text)

Enter short description of project below:

_____

_____

_____

_____ , _____ :
Client Name (CAP and bold and UL)   Location (normal text)

Enter short description of project below:

_____

_____

_____

_____ , _____ :
Client Name (CAP and bold and UL)   Location (normal text)

Enter short description of project below:

_____

_____

_____

_____ , (19___ to 19___)
Job Title (CAPS)

_____ , _____
Company Name (bold and underline)   Company Location (normal text)

Enter Job Description Below:

_____

_____

_____

_____

Accomplishments:

* _____

* _____

* _____

* _____

_____ , (19___ to 19___)
Job Title (CAPS)

_____ , _____
Company Name (bold and underline)   Company Location (normal text)

Enter Job Description Below:

_____
_____
_____
_____
_____

Accomplishments:
*
* _____
* _____
* _____

_____ , (19___ to 19___)
Job Title (CAPS)

_____ , _____
Company Name (bold and underline)   Company Location (normal text)

Enter Job Description Below:

_____
_____
_____
_____
_____

Accomplishments:
*
* _____
* _____
* _____

EDUCATION

_____ , _____
School Name (CAPS)   School Location (normal)

_____ in _____ , 19_____
Degree (bold, underlined)   Major (bold, underlined)

(Honors, Awards, Special Accomplishments) _____
*
* _____

_____ , _____
School Name (CAPS)   School Location (normal)

_____ in _____ , 19_____
Degree (bold, underlined)   Major (bold, underlined)

(Honors, Awards, Special Accomplishments) _____
*
* _____

Professional Development Courses include: _____

_____
_____
_____

PROFESSIONAL ORGANIZATIONS/CERTIFICATIONS/ PUBLICATIONS/OTHER FRILLS (choose one)

_____
_____
_____
_____
_____
_____

INTERESTS/ACTIVITITES

_____
_____
_____

References provided upon request.

STUDENT RESUME

_____
Your Name (CAPS)

_____
Your Street Address

_____
Your City, State, and Zip Code

_____
Your Phone Number

HIGHLIGHTS

- _____
- _____
- _____

EDUCATION

_____ , _____
School Name (CAPS)   School Location (normal)

_____ in _____ , 19____
Degree (bold, underlined)   Major (bold, underlined)

Honors

* _____
* _____
* _____

Student Activities
(optional)

_____
_____
_____

Relevant Courses
(optional)

_____
_____
_____
_____
_____

Internship(s):
(optional)

_____ , (_____)
Internship Job Title (CAPS)   Dates

_____ , _____
Agency/Company Name (CAPS)   Location (normal text)

Describe internship, with accomplishments, below:

_____
_____
_____
_____

_____ , (_____)
Internship Job Title (CAPS)   Dates

_____ , _____
Agency/Company Name (CAPS)   Location (normal text)

Describe internship, with accomplishments, below:

_____
_____
_____
_____

WORK EXPERIENCE _____ , _____
Company Name (CAPS)   Company Location (normal text)

_____ , (19___ to 19___)
Job Title (optional/underlined)

Enter Job Description Below:

_____
_____
_____
_____

Accomplishments:
● _____
● _____

_____ , _____
Company Name (CAPS)   Company Location (normal text)

_____ , (19___ to 19___)
Job Title (optional/underlined)

Enter Job Description Below:

_____
_____
_____
_____

Accomplishments:
● _____
● _____

_____ , _____
Company Name (CAPS)   Company Location (normal text)

_____ , (19___ to 19___)
Job Title (optional/underlined)

Enter Job Description Below:

_____
_____
_____
_____

Accomplishments:
● _____
● _____

ACTIVITIES/
INTERESTS/
FRILLS
(choose one)

_____
_____
_____
_____

REFERENCES   Provided upon request.

ARTIST/PERFORMER/WRITER RESUME

_____
Your Name (CAPS)

_____
Your Address

_____
Your Phone Number

SUMMARY

_____
_____
_____
_____

MAJOR EXHIBITIONS/PERFORMANCES/PUBLICATIONS _(choose one)_

● _____
  _____
● _____
  _____
● _____
  _____
● _____
  _____
● _____
  _____

HONORS/AWARDS

* _____
* _____
* _____
* _____
* _____

WORK HISTORY

_____ , (19___ to 19___)
Job Title (CAPS)

_____ , _____
Company Name (bold and underline)   Company Location (normal text)

Enter Job Description Below:

_____
_____
_____
_____

Accomplishments:

* _____

* _____

* _____

_____ , (19____ to 19____)

Job Title (CAPS)

_____ , _____

Company Name (bold and underline)   Company Location (normal text)

Enter Job Description Below:

_____

_____

_____

_____

Accomplishments:

* _____

* _____

* _____

_____ , (19____ to 19____)

Job Title (CAPS)

_____ , _____

Company Name (bold and underline)   Company Location (normal text)

Enter Job Description Below:

_____

_____

_____

_____

Accomplishments:

* _____

* _____

* _____

_____ , (19____ to 19____)

Job Title (CAPS)

_____ , _____

Company Name (bold and underline)   Company Location (normal text)

Enter Job Description Here

_____

_____

_____

Accomplishments (*optional*):

* _____

* _____

_____ , (19___ to 19___)
Job Title (CAPS)

_____ , _____
Company Name (bold and underline)   Company Location (normal text)

Enter Job Description Below:

_____
_____
_____
_____

EDUCATION

_____ , _____
School Name (CAPS)   School Location (normal)

_____ in _____ , 19_____
Degree (bold, underlined)   Major (bold, underlined)

(Honors, Awards, Special Accomplishments) _____
* _____
* _____

_____ , _____
School Name (CAPS)   School Location (normal)

_____ in _____ , 19_____
Degree (bold, underlined)   Major (bold, underlined)

(Honors, Awards, Special Accomplishments) _____
* _____
* _____

Special Training: _____
_____
_____
_____

PROFESSIONAL ORGANIZATIONS/CERTIFICATIONS/
SPECIAL SKILLS/OTHER FRILLS (choose one)

_____
_____
_____
_____

ACTIVITITES

_____
_____
_____
_____

References provided upon request.

TOO MANY YEARS IN SAME JOB RESUME

Your Name (CAPS)

Your Street Address

Your City, State, and Zip Code

Your Phone Number

HIGHLIGHTS

- _____
- _____
- _____
- _____
- _____

PROFESSIONAL EXPERIENCE:

_____ , _____
Company Name (CAPS and bold)   Company Location (normal text)

_____ , (19___ to 19___)
Title of Current Position (bold and underlined)   Dates of current position

_____
Area of Responsibility #1 (e.g., Administration, Sales, etc./CAPS, bold, underlined)

Enter achievements/duties within this area of responsibility below:

- _____
- _____
- _____
- _____
- _____
- _____

_____
Area of Responsibility #2 (CAPS, bold, and underlined)

Enter achievements/duties within this area of responsibility below:

- _____
- _____
- _____
- _____
- _____
- _____

Area of Responsibility #3 (CAPS, bold, and underlined)

Enter achievements/duties within this area of responsibility below:

● _____
● _____
● _____
● _____
● _____

Area of Responsibility #4 (CAPS, bold, and underlined)

Enter achievements/duties within this area of responsibility below:

● _____
● _____
● _____
● _____

Previous Positions Include: *(indicate prior positions within company)*

_____ , (19___ to 19___)
Job Title

_____ , (19___ to 19___)
Job Title

_____ , (19___ to 19___)
Job Title

_____ , _____
Previous Company Name (bold and underline)   Company Location (normal text)

Enter Job Description Below:

_____
_____
_____
_____
_____

Accomplishments:

* _____
* _____
* _____

_____ , (19___ to 19___)
Job Title (CAPS)

_____ , _____
Previous Company Name (bold and underline)   Company Location (normal text)

Enter Job Description Below:

_____
_____
_____
_____

Accomplishments:

* _____
* _____
* _____

_____ , (19___ to 19___)
Job Title (CAPS)

_____ , _____
Company Name (bold and underline)   Company Location (normal text)

Enter Job Description Below:

_____
_____
_____
_____

EDUCATION

_____ , _____
School Name (CAPS)   School Location (normal)

_____ in _____ , 19_____
Degree (bold, underlined)   Major (bold, underlined)

(Honors, Awards, Special Accomplishments) _____
* _____
* _____
   _____

_____ , _____
School Name (CAPS)   School Location (normal)

_____ in _____ , 19_____
Degree (bold, underlined)   Major (bold, underlined)

(Honors, Awards, Special Accomplishments) _____
* _____
* _____
   _____

Professional Development Courses: _____
_____
_____

PROFESSIONAL ORGANIZATIONS/CERTIFICATIONS/ SPECIAL SKILLS/OTHER FRILLS (choose one)

_____
_____
_____
_____
_____

INTERESTS/ACTIVITITES

_____
_____
_____
_____

References provided upon request.

CAREER CHANGER/SPECIAL PROBLEMS RESUME

_____
Your Name (CAPS)

_____
Your Street Address

_____
Your City, State, and Zip Code

_____
Your Phone Number

JOB OBJECTIVE

_____
_____
_____

AREAS OF EXPERTISE (SKILLS)

_____
Write name of first skill category here (lowercase bold and UL)

- _____
- _____
- _____
- _____
- _____
- _____

_____
Write name of second skill category here (lowercase bold and UL)

- _____
- _____
- _____
- _____
- _____
- _____

_____
Write name of third skill category here (lowercase bold and UL)

- _____
- _____
- _____
- _____
- _____

RELEVANT EXPERIENCE:

(NOTE: Move the Education section here, above Relevant Experience, if your educational background is stronger than your work experience.)

_____ , (19___ to 19___)
Job/Internship//Volunteer Work Title (bold and CAPS)

_____ , _____
Company Name (Bold and underlined)   Company Location (normal text)

Enter Job Description Below:

_____
_____
_____
_____
_____

Accomplishments:

* _____
* _____
* _____

_____ , (19___ to 19___)
Job/Internship//Volunteer Work Title (bold and CAPS)

_____ , _____
Company Name (Bold and underlined)   Company Location (normal text)

Enter Job Description Below:

_____
_____
_____
_____
_____

Accomplishments:

* _____
* _____
* _____

_____ , (19___ to 19___)
Job/Internship//Volunteer Work Title (bold and CAPS)

_____ , _____
Company Name (Bold and underlined)   Company Location (normal text)

Enter Job Description Below:

_____
_____
_____
_____

OTHER EXPERIENCE/PREVIOUS EXPERIENCE/WORK HISTORY

_____ , (19___ to 19___)
Job Title (CAPS)

_____ , _____
Company Name (Bold and underlined)   Company Location (normal text)
Enter Job Description Below:

_____
_____
_____
_____
_____

_____ , (19___ to 19___)
Job Title (CAPS)

_____ , _____
Previous Company Name (bold and underline)   Company Location (normal text)

Enter Job Description Below:

_____
_____
_____
_____

_____ , (19___ to 19___)
Job Title (CAPS)

_____ , _____
Company Name (bold and underline)   Company Location (normal text)

Enter Job Description Below:

_____
_____
_____
_____

EDUCATION

_____ ,   _____
School Name (CAPS)   School Location (normal)
_____ in _____ , 19_____
Degree (bold, underlined)   Major (bold, underlined)

(Honors, Awards, Special Accomplishments) _____
*
* _____
_____

_____ ,   _____
School Name (CAPS)   School Location (normal)
_____ in _____ , 19_____
Degree (bold, underlined)   Major (bold, underlined)

(Honors, Awards, Special Accomplishments) _____
*
* _____
_____

Professional Development Courses: _____
_____
_____

PROFESSIONAL ORGANIZATIONS/CERTIFICATIONS/
HONORS/OTHER FRILLS (choose one)

_____
_____
_____
_____
_____

INTERESTS/ACTIVITITES

_____
_____
_____
_____

References provided upon request.

APPENDIX 2

SAMPLE RESUMES

LESLIE WHITLA
77 Meredown Street, Apt. 11
Syosset, New York 11234
516-682-7901

CERTIFIED PUBLIC ACCOUNTANT

HIGHLIGHTS

- Extensive background in both public and private accounting.
- Special expertise in tax analysis and preparation at corporate, partnership, trust, and individual levels.
- Know numerous tax software packages including COMPUTAX, Prentice-Hall, FAST, and Lotus 1-2-3.
- Management and supervisory experience.
- Master's Degree in Taxation from Bentley College; C.P.A. 1988.

WORK HISTORY

Public Accounting

SENIOR TAX ACCOUNTANT (1987 to Present)
Chase & Silver, New York, NY

Analyzed corporate returns prepared by junior and senior staff for tax compliance and accuracy. Addressed and resolved special problems. Prepared and reviewed individual returns during tax season; prepared individual tax projections. Performed review and compilation services.

Accomplishments:

- Improved speed and efficiency of Tax Department by 300%, receiving special commendation from superiors.
- Consistently received superior evaluations.

SENIOR ACCOUNTANT (1984 to 1987)
Downing, Walters & Company, New York, NY
Provided audit services for large corporations including Somerville Lumber. Performed reviews and compilations. Prepared tax returns for individuals, trusts, and partnerships. Analyzed client investments and prepared quarterly reports.

Accomplishments:

- Earned C.P.A. License in State of Massachusetts.
- Consistently received superior evaluations.

STAFF ACCOUNTANT (1983 to 1984)
Howard, Smith, Davey & Company, New York, NY
Prepared federal and state tax returns for corporations and individuals. Performed review and compilation services. Performed general accounting services for clients.

Private Accounting

GENERAL ACCOUNTANT (1981 to 1982)
Polymer Ready Plastics, Inc., Jamaica, NY
Prepared federal and state income tax returns. Developed audit workpapers for outside auditors. Prepared monthly financial statements.

LESLIE WHITLA
Page 2

ASSISTANT TO VICE-PRESIDENT OF FINANCE (1977-80)
The Management Center, Inc., Flushing, NY
Generated monthly accruals and financial statements. Supervised and trained accounts payable and receivable clerks. Completed performance evaluations. Maintained computerized payroll system.

EDUCATION   BENTLEY COLLEGE, Waltham, MA
Master of Science Degree in Taxation (1983)

HOFSTRA UNIVERSITY, Garden City, NY
Bachelor of Science Degree in Accounting

REFERENCES   Available upon request.

ACCOUNT EXECUTIVE
Sample One-Page Resume

WINSTON T. PAULSON
42 Andover Road
Reading, MA 02365
(617)742-8939

WORK EXPERIENCE

RASTON, INC., Lowell, MA (1988-Present)
Account Executive
Implement account development and account penetration for a client base of 200+ that includes such major corporations as Digital, New England Telephone, and State Street Bank. Present and sell Raston products and custom graphics services. Open new departments within client base.

Increased revenue in territory by 32% in last two quarters.

THE MARKETING GROUP, INC., Houston, Texas (1986-1988)
Sales/Marketing Manager
Oversaw marketing and sales of four-color newsletters and follow-up products for real estate professionals. Hired and trained sales personnel and supervised a staff of 14. Utilized direct mail, telecommunications, magazine advertising, videotapes, and presentations at seminars and conventions to market newsletters throughout the United States and Canada. Dealt with corporate directors, brokers, agents of franchise, independent real estate operators, investors, and mortgage companies.

Instrumental in starting up telemarketing department.

SULLIVAN & YODER, INC., Des Moines, Iowa (1985-1986)
Account Executive
Oversaw day-to-day operations and coordinated three major consumer and retail accounts. Secured new business, including the Iowa Lottery account. Conducted market research and coordinated media planning, print and broadcast advertising and public relations. Assessed client needs and structured appropriate advertising programs.

BENTON & BOWLES, INC., Houston, Texas (1981-1985)
Account Executive
Worked with account supervisor on Texas Commerce Bank. Assisted with marketing plans and presented print, collateral, and broadcast jobs to the client.

Traffic Manager
Initiated traffic system at B&B. Coordinated all broadcast, print, and collateral jobs through all departments. Secondary print production, small print jobs, duplicate film orders, and print and broadcasting estimating. Promoted to Account Executive.

BRANDON ADVERTISING, INC., Houston, Texas (1980-1981)
Traffic-Production Assistant
Coordinated all print and collateral jobs through agency. Assisted production manager with print estimating.

EDUCATION

C.W. Post/Long Island University
Bachelor of Arts in Journalism, 1980
Wellesley College, Wellesley, MA (1976-1978)

REFERENCES

Available upon request

```
┌─────────────────────────────┐
│ BANK MANAGER                │
│ Sample Resume               │
└─────────────────────────────┘
```

JOANNE MCCARTHY
111 Praline Street, Allston, MA 01513   (617) 247-6097

Bank Management Professional

SUMMARY

Nine years of community banking experience, with strong background in management, customer relations, and investment counseling.

PROFESSIONAL EXPERIENCE

1981-Present

SHAWMUT BANK

Held progressively responsible positions in various Shawmut branches. **Promoted 10 times in 9 years** to current position as:

Customer Service Manager/Floating Manager (10/86-Present)

Manage operations, service, and sales of the Hingham Plaza Branch office of Shawmut Bank. As Floating Manager, provide management and customer service consultation to numerous branch banks.

- **Counsel customers on investment options,** including discount brokerage services, certificates of deposit, money market/savings accounts, trust services, treasury bill investments, IRAs, and retirement plans.

- **Pre-qualify customers** for mortgages.

- **Recruit and supervise staff,** conduct performance reviews, offer career guidance.

- **Motivate staff** to excel in sales.

- **Develop new accounts** through calling on local corporations and businesses.

- **Set branch policy,** oversee administration, manage community relations.

Community Banking Management Program (1/86-10/86)

Selected out of a pool of hundreds of Shawmut Bank employees to participate in this ten-month, full-time management training program. Completed intensive program of classroom training combined with experience working in all bank departments (Operations, Brokerage Services, Trust Department, Mortgage Underwriting, Security, Etc.).

JOANNE MCCARTHY
Page 2

Previous Positions At Shawmut Bank:

- Senior Service Representative for Region II (1985)
- Certified Senior Sales Representative (1984)
- Certified Customer Assistance Representative (1984)
- Floating Customer Service Representative (1982-84)
- Customer Service Representative (1981-82)

Achievements:

At top of class in management training program (1986).

Achieved top sales of all Customer Service Representatives in all Shawmut Banks (1984).

Awarded perfect (10) ratings for service and operations (1983-85).

Received numerous letters of commendation for outstanding service to customers (1986 - present).

EDUCATION

1986	<u>Management training program</u>, Shawmut Bank Completed advanced courses in accounting, personnel administration, marketing, and all aspects of management.
1982-84	<u>Boston University</u> Major in Business Administration
1977-80	<u>University of Vermont</u> Associates Degree in Business Administration with a concentration in **Economics.**

ACTIVITIES

Board of Directors, Cambridge YMCA (1987-Present)

Guest Lecturer, University of New Hampshire (1988) "Careers in Banking and Loans" (Small Business Management Program)

Member, Masters National Swim Team

Apprentice to renowned potter Amy Jameson

REFERENCES   Provided upon request.

CAREER/ACADEMIC COUNSELOR
Sample Resume

NANCY CARAN
34-12 Duck Run Drive
Milton, NJ 07526
(516) 766-4444

SUMMARY OF QUALIFICATIONS

Masters-level counselor, with considerable experience in academic, career, and personal counseling, and specialized training in testing and educational psychology.

PROFESSIONAL EXPERIENCE

CAREER COUNSELOR   1990-Present
New York University, New York, NY

Advise over 300 graduate students per year about career options. Administer career assessment tests such as the Meyers-Briggs and Strong-Campbell. Provide job search guidance and lead job search skills workshops.

Achievements:

- Developed innovative series of workshops on various careers, attended by over 500 students.

- Expanded career resource library by 70%.

- Wrote complete manuals on resume writing and job search skills, distributed to all incoming graduate students.

ACADEMIC COUNSELOR   1988-1990
United Career Centers, Fort Lauderdale, FL

Administered aptitude and career assessment tests, including Meyer-Briggs, and interpreted results to students. Guided students in designing course of study based on test results and interviews. Counseled students on issues of achievement and behavioral problems affecting academic performance. Monitored attendance. Screened applicants and provided referral to outside programs when appropriate.

SERVICE COORDINATOR   1987
Nursefinders, Hollywood, FL

Interviewed and screened prospective field staff (RNs, LPNs, and CNAs). Sold services to area clients (hospitals and nursing homes). Placed field staff in various assignments. Investigated financial status of prospective clients.

FRONT DESK COUNSELOR   1985-1986
Western Connecticut State University, Danbury, CT

Monitored conduct of dormitory residents. Member of coordinating staff committee.

INTERNSHIP

HOLISTIC WELLNESS RESOURCE CENTER
Garden City, NY

Implemented and organized programming for an ongoing Holistic Wellness radio talk show. Established contacts and interviewed prospective talk show guests. Organized and co-led a wellness workshop with adolescents at the Westbury Detention Center.

NANCY CARAN
Page 2

EDUCATION

<u>Master of Science in Educational Counseling</u>
Hofstra University, Garden City, NY   May, 1990

<u>Bachelor of Arts in Psychology</u>
Western Connecticut State University, Danbury, CT   May, 1987

References furnished upon request

> **CHEF**
> Sample Resume

ALLAN G. ROSE
53 Howard Road
Greeley, Colorado 08745
(547) 675-2227

HIGHLIGHTS

- **Production expertise**
  Including menu development and planning, supervision of day-to-day operations, developing award-winning recipes.

- **Management and supervisory expertise**
  Including overseeing staff of 20, hiring and firing, managing cost and inventory control, and organizing production for volume kitchen.

- **Purchasing expertise**
  Including food and beverages, equipment, and services for volume production restaurant and catering outlets.

PROFESSIONAL EXPERIENCE

EXECUTIVE CHEF, (1989 to Present)
The Lyme Inne, Denver, Colorado
Organize and oversee all aspects of management and food production to supply the three restaurant locations and catering outlet of this kosher establishment.
- Responsible for all buying including food and beverages, equipment, tools, uniforms, chemicals, and services.
- Control substantial monthly provisions budget.
- Responsible for cost, inventory and waste control.
- Responsible for hiring, firing, and supervision of staff of 20; control monthly payroll.
- Plan and develop menus; organize and oversee daily production; direct supplying of all restaurant locations and catering department.
- Planned, developed, and directed opening of new kitchen, including development and implementation of coordinated baking system.
- Developed breads and pastries for new meat kitchen; improved and revamped baked goods restaurant-wide.
- Reduced costs by 17%.

CHEF/PASTRY CHEF, (1987 to 1989)
The Fountain, Providence, Rhode Island
Developed, produced and served full menu, from appetizers to desserts, for this unique vegetarian restaurant.
- Designed and produced complete menu.
- Developed and produced full line of desserts, including tortes, cakes, pies, tarts, pastries, and puddings.
- Responsible for all ordering, inventory, dealing with vendors, food cost management, and waste management.
- Supervised part-time kitchen staff.
- Won first place, Creative Gourmets Culinary Competition, (1989, 1990) for original recipes.

PASTRY CHEF, (1985 to 1987)
Ambles, Providence, Rhode Island
Developed and produced full line of desserts to supply Ambles' restaurant outlets and catering departments. Product line included tortes, cakes, pies, tarts, puddings, pastries (danish, croissant, eclairs), brownies, and cookies.

ALLAN G. ROSE

PASTRY CHEF, (1983 to 1984)
Rosemary's, Denver, Colorado
Produced pastries, cakes, tarts, pies, and specialty items to supply the retail and wholesale departments.

BAKER/CHOCOLATIER, (1982 to 1983)
The Chocolate Dream, Denver, Colorado
Baked scones, cakes, muffins, specialty cookies, and assisted with the production of truffles and other chocolate confections.

ASSISTANT PROFESSOR, (1979 to 1981)
The University of Colorado, Denver, CO
Designed and taught a variety of courses in the Political Science Department.

EDUCATION

Johnson & Wales College, Providence, Rhode Island
B.A. in Food Service Management, 1987
Graduated Magna Cum Laude

Ithaca College, Ithaca, NY
B.A. in Political Science, 1975

REFERENCES

Available upon request

> **CHIEF EXECUTIVE OFFICER (CEO)**
> Sample Resume

GARY S. HUMMEL
32 West Ridge Road
Portland, Maine 22389
(547) 698-4861

HIGHLIGHTS

● Proven track record developing niche businesses from start-up to multimillion dollar ventures.

● Exceptional success extricating companies from financial disaster.

● Record of successfully introducing innovative new products, marketing strategies, and management approaches.

● Outstanding record in negotiating mergers, acquisitions, and cooperative arrangements, and in merging discrete corporate cultures into a functional whole.

PROFESSIONAL EXPERIENCE

PRESIDENT and CEO
Danforth Group, Augusta, Maine (1986 to Present)
The largest U.S. company supplying entertainment and education products to schools.

Developed this niche business from start-up to an $80 million company with 3500 employees within four years. Acquired five smaller companies, conducting all market research and negotiations. Executed personnel reorganization to decentralize business. Spearhead all product development efforts. Initiate joint venture negotiations to acquire new technologies. Completed successful negotiations to develop innovative joint projects with television studios and networks. Direct strategic planning. Oversee budgets and personnel matters.

Accomplishments:

● Brought company from start-up to $80 million and 40% of total market share within four years.

● Successfully amalgamated various corporate cultures and staff.

● Developed an innovative new technology that connects televisions to a mainframe computer, allowing administration to program special items (menus, announcements, etc.) centrally.

● Introduced new program offerings, such as a drug education series.

● Created a third-party service organization.

● Currently negotiating broadcast arrangements with a satellite network; also completing negotiations with a major cable network to install televisions broadcasting information about new technologies in school offices.

VICE PRESIDENT, CORPORATE DEVELOPMENT
ACTING VICE PRESIDENT OF MARKETING
Allister Corporation, Boston, MA (1984 to 1986)
Allister Corp. is a subsidiary of ECG, one of Europe's ten largest companies.

Moved company from annual losses exceeding $100 million to break-even point within two years. Established decentralized management plan allowing company branches to function independently. Reorganized staffing. Supervised 50 staff directly. Established monthly management reporting structure. Sold unprofitable subsidiary. Initiated successful new marketing strategies. Acquired new product lines. Negotiated government contracts. Negotiated product acquisition with Japanese vendors. Developed plan to joint venture retail branches to local entrepreneurs. Reduced workforce by 15%.

GARY S. HUMMEL
Page 2

___

Accomplishments:

- Successfully extricated company from financial disaster.

- Reestablished banking relationships ($80 million) that had disintegrated.

- Established alternate capital sources ($40 million in lease financings).

- Introduced seven new product offerings — more than the company had introduced in the three previous years, including a unique new product line.

- Improved direct mail response by over 200% through innovative marketing.

- Increased dealer sales by 20% through improved promotions.

VICE PRESIDENT & CONTROLLER (1980-84)
ECG (European Corporate Group), London, England

Oversaw financial and management reporting and implementation of internal controls. Implemented a corporate MIS system. Prepared and presented financial statements and statutory filings. Sat on the Boards of subsidiary companies (Altion, CanBer Energy Resources, etc.) and oversaw financial management of subsidiaries. Met legal and audit requirements for international debt and equity financings. Evaluated and negotiated corporate acquisitions. Directly supervised 25 staff members.

Accomplishments:

- Served as Director/Officer for 15 subsidiary companies.

- Negotiated CanBer/Texas Gulf purchase with a team, completing the largest acquisition ever done in the world at that time.

- Negotiated unusual financings, including silver backed debentures and dual currency preferred shares.

PARTNER
Milte, Widdell & Co., Toronto, Ontario (1970 to 1980)
Promoted five times to this position. Started as Articulating Student, 1970.

Supervised students and accountants in corporate audit activities. Ensured that financial statements of all clients met applicable standards. Assumed responsibility for several large accounts, including ECG. Taught at the School of Accountancy run by the Ontario Institute of Chartered Accountants.

EDUCATION

RYERSON POLYTECHNICAL INSTITUTE, Toronto
Bachelor of Business Administration, 1973
Graduated third in class of 300.

CANADIAN INSTITUTE OF CHARTERED ACCOUNTANTS
Granted CA (CPA equivalent) 1975.
Scored 12th highest in all of Canada.

MEMBERSHIPS/ACTIVITIES

- Member of the President's Organization
- Member of the Northeastern University Advisory Council
- Member of the Financial Executive's Institute of Boston
- Member of the Conference Board
- Member of Chartered Accountants of Ontario

Enjoy tennis, skiing, swimming

CONFERENCE
COORDINATOR
Sample Resume

ALLISON RUSH
50 Shackley Street
Fitchburg, Massachusetts 11520
(508) 265-7760

PROFESSIONAL EXPERTISE

Events Coordination

- Arranging conference logistics for events attended by up to 600 people. Securing conference facilities, arranging meals, procuring equipment and handling equipment failures.
- Overseeing publicity. Designing and producing brochures, writing marketing letters, developing catalogs and posters, creating advertisements for print media.
- Developing registration procedures and tracking systems.
- Engaging speakers and workshop leaders.
- Planning full roster of activities, including both topical workshops and recreational activities.
- Recruiting and supervising volunteer staff.

Arts Management

- Managing all aspects of freelance design business.
- Providing graphic design, calligraphy, and chair caning services.

Recreational Therapy

- Extensive background in gerontology, including experience providing private elder home care and recreational therapy for groups of up to 200.
- Degree in Psychology, with 3.3 average in major subjects. Post-graduate coursework at Boston University and Middlesex Community College.
- Experience as Teaching Assistant for Introductory Psychology courses.

WORK HISTORY

RUSH GRAPHICS, Fitchburg, MA (1983 to Present)
Special Events Coordinator
Arrange all special events for this enterprise providing graphic design, calligraphy, and silkscreening services to the public. Develop marketing materials, keep financial records and allocate budget, purchase equipment and supplies. Arrange accommodations and refreshments with outside vendors. Recruit speakers and presenters. Annual events include:

Exhibition of The Cabinetmakers of Fitchburg. Conceived and organized this highly successful fundraising event attended by over 600 people. Recruited 25 volunteers, coordinated publicity and mailings, wrote press releases and grants. Designed exhibits, organized opening reception with music, solicited donations for catered food, time, and money from individuals and merchants.

Block Island Conference (Block Island, RI). Co-chaired this three-day conference attended by 350 people. Secured facility and caterers. Designed program. Recruited speakers and workshop leaders. Organized recreational activities including a full-scale triathlon. Publicized event, including designing brochure, developing mailing lists, and writing marketing letters. Coordinated registration. Supervised volunteer staff of 70. Developed special children's program.

Parade, Stell Farm Historical Association (Fitchburg). Organized parade. Solicited donations from community organizations. Designed and built parade float, supervising committee of eight.

ALLISON RUSH
Page 2

FREELANCE EVENTS COORDINATOR (1981 to Present)
Coordinated and directed all arrangements for parties, weddings, and special events for up to 150 people. Worked with numerous clients.

CENTRAL MASS FOOD COOP, Gardner, MA (Part-Time/1985-1988)
Co-Coordinator
Managed all operations of this food coop serving 40 families. Recruited new members. Recruited volunteer staff, delegated responsibilities and provided supervision. Called meetings of the Board of Directors and set policy. Oversaw daily operations and facility maintenance. Found new suppliers and expanded product lines. Organized special events.

PRIVATE ELDER HOME CARE (1982-83)
Provided support services to homebound elderly individuals. Coordinated services with medical professionals and family members. Offered crisis intervention.

LEO IRVINE REHABILITATION CENTER FOR THE AGED, Roslindale, MA (1980-81)
Recreational Therapist
Planned special events for approximately 200 residents. Designed daily programs for groups of 5-25 severely brain-damaged residents. Taught and supervised student interns.

COMMUNITY ACTIVITIES

Co-Chair, Parent Education Committee, Gardner-Tow School, Fitchburg, MA (1989)
Arranged speaker series. Called and chaired meetings. Directed activities.

Treasurer, Worcester Waldorf Nursery School, Worcester, MA (1987-88)
Oversaw annual budget. Tracked and delegated funds.

EDUCATION

UNIVERSITY OF ROCHESTER, Rochester, NY
Bachelor of Arts in Psychology. *3.5 average in major subjects.*
Dean's List every semester of last two years.

POST-GRADUATE COURSES in gerontology, business management, arts, and dance at Boston University, Fitchburg State College, and the DeCordova Museum.

INTERESTS

Offer freelance classical singing in the Renaissance style. Speak French. Enjoy aerobics, photography, costume making, and graphics.

REFERENCES

Provided upon request.

CORRECTIONS OFFICER
Sample Resume

ROGER STEVENS
58 Third Avenue
Pittsburgh, PA 36988
(268)652-4881

SUMMARY

Over 18 years of experience in all phases of Security, including building security systems and equipment; security and weapons checks; supervision of security personnel and inmates; transportation of inmates and dangerous personnel; qualified on 38 caliber revolver, shotgun, and restraint equipment; training provider for new Correction Officers.

PROFESSIONAL EXPERIENCE

CORRECTIONS OFFICER/SERGEANT
Pennsylvania Correctional Institution, Pittsburgh (1972-Present)
Conduct all aspects of prison security including: supervision and training of correction officers, overseeing security of buildings and grounds, and supervising inmates for these maximum security (Pittsburgh) and medium security (Reading) facilities housing up to 1200 inmates.

- Assign tasks to correction officers; supervise officers in security checks, guard details, movement of inmates, assignment of work details to inmates, and other prison activities; coordinate security crews; and supervise inmates by monitoring their activities and living quarters, assigning and overseeing work details, checking for weapons and security risks, administering restraint and discipline, etc.

- Qualified to oversee security in all prison areas including new line, can, wall towers, outer control, inner control, mail room, yards, shops, cell blocks, and entire buildings.

- Supervise up to 500 inmates, and up to 50 officers, depending on station.

- Interact with PCI administration, court officials, medical and psychological personnel, clergy, other law enforcement officers, and the public as required by assignment.

- Carry out weapon and security checks, write reports.

Achievements
- Selected as **Acting Shift Commander** (equivalent to rank of Acting Captain) on five occasions, with responsibility for running entire institution.

- Selected as **Acting Supervisor** (equivalent to rank of acting Lieutenant) on more than 50 occasions, with responsibility for running entire sections of the institution.

- Promoted to **Senior Correction Officer**, April, 1983.

- **Commendation from the Superintendent, Midlantic Correctional Center,** for capture and return of escapee on August 21, 1982.

- **Trainer** for new correction officers on transportation of inmates.

RENDITION OFFICER
State Transportation, Pennsylvania Department of Correction (1986-1989)
Responsible for all phases of transportation of inmates to locations within and outside of the state.

- Arranged and implemented secure transportation of inmates to medical and legal appointments, transfers, etc., using cruiser and van.

- Arranged and implemented rendition of escapees within and outside of the state, using police cruiser and major airlines. Applied restraint equipment.

- Interacted with local and state police and airport security to arrange for secure transport of inmates.

ROGER STEVENS
Page 2

Achievements

- **Commendation from the Deputy Director of Transportation**, for response to a riot and transporting 136 inmates to other maximum security facilities around the state on August 26, 1988.

- **Commendation from the Superintendent, PCI Pittsburgh**, for professionalism in retrieving prisoners in a pre-release facility and returning them to maximum security institutions on December 29 and 30, 1987.

- **Commendation from Department of Transportation**, for assistance beyond the call of duty to civilians in an emergency on July 31, 1987.

EDUCATION

Numerous professional courses and workshops including:

- Forty-Hour Inservice Training Program, PCI

- First Line Supervisory Program

- DOC Transportation Policies and Procedures

- Qualification for Weapons - 38 caliber revolver and shotgun

- Stress Awareness Program

- Advanced Correction Officer Practice

- Report Writing

References available upon request.

DENTAL ASSISTANT
Sample One-Page Resume

ESTHER J. LEIBVITZ
57 Park Circle
Mill Valley, CA 22143
(557) 549-4345

SUMMARY

Dental Assistant with more than eleven years of experience. Thorough knowledge of four-handed dentistry, with superior technical skills and excellent record in maintaining good patient relations.

BUSINESS EXPERIENCE

Richard Tracy, D.M.D., Novato, CA
DENTAL ASSISTANT   1985 to 1989
Providing a wide range of assistant functions in this busy four-handed dentistry practice.
- Took alginate impressions; poured and trimmed models.
- Assisted with crown and bridge, including hydrocolloid, rubber-based, and impergum impressions; packing cord; selecting shade.
- Made temporaries and cemented in patients' mouths. Removed excess cement.
- Removed temporaries and placed permanent crowns.
- Took, developed, and mounted X-rays.
- Mixed fillings and bonding.
- Assisted in endo and extractions.
- Cleaned and sterilized instruments.
- Ordered and stocked medical supplies for office.
- Supervised case shipment and receipt from lab.

Accomplishments
- Assumed double workload several days each week.
- Commended for technical skills.
- Maintained excellent patient relations.

L. Miller, D.M.D. and T. Segwick, D.D.S., Mill Valley, CA
DENTAL ASSISTANT   1985
Provided general dental assistance in this two-dentist practice of renowned prosthodontists.

Roger Goldman, Mill Valley, CA
DENTAL ASSISTANT   1978 to 1985
Sole assistant in this general dentistry practice.

PREVIOUS EXPERIENCE

Airline stewardess for American Airlines for several years. Five years previous experience as a dental assistant (Community Dentists, San Francisco).

SPECIAL TRAINING

Courses at MARLO CLINIC, SAN FRANCISCO STATE COLLEGE, and REED COLLEGE (1977-79) including C.P.R., Vital Signs and Medical History, Radiology for Dental Auxiliary.

ACTIVITIES

Member, Rocky Mountain Club. Climbed several 4000 ft. peaks (Mt. Webster, Mt. Jackson). Acted in several community productions.

REFERENCES

Available upon request

```
┌─────────────────────────┐
│ DISTRICT SALES MANAGER  │
│ Sample Resume           │
└─────────────────────────┘
```

DANIELLE A. MACDONALD
19 Grover Circle
Framingham, MA 61732
(798) 339-5983

SUMMARY OF QUALIFICATIONS

District Sales Manager with proven track record in developing and managing new territories, opening new accounts, building long-term customer relations, and increasing profit margins substantially. Special expertise includes technical skills in graphics, printing, and computers.

PROFESSIONAL EXPERIENCE

DISTRICT SALES MANAGER
A. Stevens Company, Inc., Boston, MA (1978 - Present)
A custom folding carton and set-up box manufacturer with headquarters in Teaneck, N.J.

Developed new sales territory (New England). Researched prospects, developed target market lists; secured new accounts in an extremely competitive market. Set up new office. Advise customers' graphic designers, product development teams, and scheduling teams on product design issues in order to develop individualized solutions that are both cost-effective and manufacturable. Coordinate production from concept to manufacture.

Accomplishments:

- Averaged more new accounts (1978 to present) than any other sales representative in the company.

- Received Commendation for opening the second largest number of new accounts in 1989.

- Received Golden Award for developing the most new accounts in the company (1985, 1986, 1987).

- Received Company Award for producing the third largest volume of business in 1986.

PRODUCT DEVELOPMENT - MARKETING MANAGER
International Headquarters, Norwalk Corporation, Lansing, Michigan (1977-78)

Coordinated a product development team that developed environmentally safe personal care products and containers. Analyzed competitive products. Recommended packaging solutions and product formulas; coordinated efforts of chemists and engineers. Prepared extensive reports recommending product alterations. Suggested new product lines; coordinated positioning of new and existing products. Oversaw product testing.

Accomplishments:

- Initiated promotional campaigns that increased sales up to 30%.

- Oversaw $26MM annual product sales.

ACCOUNT EXECUTIVE
Alphanetic Corporation, Detroit, Michigan (1976-77)

Developed individualized sales forecasting systems for large accounts including Westinghouse Electric and Clark Equipment Corporation, utilizing an IBM mainframe computer. Employed macroeconomic modeling — tracking sales and correlating to projected economic factors over a five-year period. Secured new accounts.

DANIELLE A. MACDONALD
Page 2

Accomplishments:

- Achieved 95% prediction accuracy in all sales projections systems developed.

- Increased revenue by $200,000; secured three major new accounts and extended existing accounts.

SALES REPRESENTATIVE
Design Center of America, Grand Rapids, Michigan (1974-76)

Selected as trainee for one-year sales management program providing training in all aspects of the manufacturing, sales, customer service, and pre-press operations. After completing program, developed new territory in Ohio, selling printing and packaging services.

Accomplishments:

- Doubled sales in Ohio territory in one-and-a-half year period to $650M.

ASSISTANT DIRECTOR/MEMBER OF THE FACULTY
University of Michigan Scottish Highlanders (1971-74)
Paid for 70% of own college education with salary from this position.

Managed 56 members of this all-womens' bagpipe band, plus 70 students-in-training. Scheduled performances at Big Ten sporting events; coordinated rehearsals; made travel arrangements. Provided musical instruction to individual students and furnished overall musical direction for the band.

EDUCATION

BACHELOR'S DEGREE IN BUSINESS ADMINISTRATION
University of Michigan, 1974
Majors in Marketing and Management.

CONTINUING EDUCATION COURSES
Lansing Community College, Lansing, MI (1980-84)

SPECIAL SKILLS

Graphics expertise, including technical skills in film and color separation; pre-press functions; color-matching; specialty coating; package conversion; and all forms of printing, die-cutting, and leaf-stamping equipment.

Computer expertise, including knowledge of programming in BASIC and FORTRAN; Systems Analysis; and Stat Pak.

REFERENCES

Provided upon request.

ELECTRICAL ENGINEER
Sample Resume

DAVID GONZALEZ

57 Lexington Road   Home: (554) 443-5544
Derby, Kentucky 22392   Work: (554) 455-6598

OBJECTIVES   A position in engineering management utilizing both my expertise in team leadership and background in analog circuit engineering.

EDUCATION   RENSSELAER POLYTECHNIC INSTITUTE, Troy, New York
Bachelor of Science in Electrical Engineering, 1986

Honors:
- Outstanding Recognition Award, Society of Hispanic Professional Engineers.
- Dean's List of Distinguished Students.
- Received Rensselaer Scholarship and Bridge Scholarship.
- President, Latin Students Association.
- Chairman, Society of Hispanic Professional Engineers.

PROFESSIONAL EXPERIENCE

1987 to Present   Irok Systems, Ranford, Kentucky
COMPONENT/APPLICATIONS ENGINEER

Provide technical assistance to design engineers in the selection and application of all electrical parts used in Itek Systems-designed equipment (particularly, state-of-the-art semiconductor and microcircuit devices). Develop, disseminate, and enforce derating rules. Evaluate new parts and technologies to determine potential for use. Perform application evaluation of commercial devices intended for military use. Provide physical and electrical characterization of discrete components to establish device modeling database. Initiate analysis of new vendor parts and processes. Develop testing techniques, perform failure analyses, and recommend corrective action for new parts and materials from both factory and field.

Achievements
- APPOINTED TASK ENGINEER for the AMRAAM Program. Managed group of engineers and technicians. Assigned tasks, set deadlines, monitored progress of project, led weekly meetings, assumed ultimate responsibility for the Program within the Product Assurance Lab.

- APPOINTED COORDINATOR of the Phoenix Missile Investigation Requests Group within the Laboratory.

- COORDINATED the Product Assurance Microwave Semiconductor Microcircuit Engineering Group for APREP Missile Program.

- PRODUCED IN-DEPTH DOCUMENTATION of design practices and procedures within the Product Assurance Laboratory, for use in technical manuals. Established cost estimates and schedules, compiled list of potential replacement parts, reviewed new qualifications, etc.

- LED FAILURE ANALYSIS GROUP investigating failure of a line receiver in the Patriot Missile Group System.

- GENERATED DRAWINGS used in the development of microwave monolithic integrated circuit.

1986   Northern Telecom Electronics, Electronics Components Group
West Palm Beach, Florida

TEST ENGINEER/PRODUCTION SUPERVISOR
Developed software and set up laser systems for the passive, parametric, and active trimming of purely resistive networks as well as products with active components and prototypes. Assigned to be Prime Leader for trim operations of two products with significant impact on Hybrid manufacturing. Oversaw development of software used to implement test equipment for passive products. Assisted in design of resistive networks using thick film and laser-trimming concepts. Supervised hybrid production, testing, and quality control.

1986 (Summer)   Construction Implementation and Procedures, Miami, Florida

ELECTRICAL ENGINEER
Acted as Assistant Project Manager to oversee the remodeling and development of a branch bank in South Florida. Supervised all electrical installations and performed related administrative tasks.

1985 (Summer)   Proctor and Gamble Paper Products Company, Mehoopany, Pennsylvania

ELECTRICAL ENGINEER
Managed projects involving design and implementation of energy-saving procedures, quality control, and re-application.

OTHER EXPERIENCE

1984 (Summer)   Harvard University, Upward Bound Program, Cambridge, MA

TUTOR/COUNSELOR
Tutored seventy high school students in mathematics, physics, and English.

SPECIAL SKILLS

- Know FORTRAN, WATFIV, Computer Graphics, BASIC, and SNOBOL.
- Bilingual in English and Spanish.

REFERENCES

Available upon request

> **GROCERY MANAGER**
> Sample Resume

RAYMOND SZECIEK
10 Greenbriar Road, Orlando, FL 61603   (407) 473-1569

===

SUMMARY

- Grocery manager with considerable experience supervising and training staff and overseeing all operations of several departments.

- Expertise in buying, including negotiating with vendors and minimizing back-stock.

- Special interest in the food industry.

WORK HISTORY

1982-Present

FOURSTAR MARKET, Orlando, FL

<u>Assistant **Grocery Manager**</u> (1988-90)

Manage four departments that together generate about 40% of the store's revenue: Frozen Foods, Dairy, General Merchandise, and Commercial Bakery. Supervise staff, review staff performance, recommend promotions and raises. Order all merchandise, suggest retail prices, bring in new lines of merchandise, and insure that correct amounts of inventory are stocked. Create sales displays.

Accomplishments:

- Act as Night Manager on rotating basis, assuming responsibility for all store operations.

- Decreased back-stock considerably since 1986.

- Improved diversity of product offerings, effectiveness of displays, and customer satisfaction.

- Received consistently excellent performance evaluations.

- Promoted five times in eight years.

<u>**Frozen Food/Dairy Manager**</u> (1984-88)

Supervised all operations of these two departments. Answered customer questions. Bought all merchandise. Made sure that items were properly stocked and displayed.

<u>**Previous Positions:**</u>

- Receiver, 1984
- Floor Person (part-time), 1984
- Cashier (part-time) 1982-83

MUSIC EXPERIENCE

Compose and perform original compositions for voice and guitar. Performances to date include:

<u>The **Rounder Coffeehouse**</u> (Orlando, FL). Four appearances in 1990.

<u>The **Homegrown**</u> (Miami, FL). One appearance in 1989.

EDUCATION

FLORIDA STATE UNIVERSITY, 1987-90
General studies, Math, English

REFERENCES

Available upon request.

HORTICULTURIST/
LANDSCAPE DESIGNER
Sample Resume

LORRAINE T. ADAMS
95 Water Road
Burlington, MA 01875
(617) 297-6279

SUMMARY

HORTICULTURIST/LANDSCAPE DESIGNER with extensive background advising customers on plant care, design, and maintenance.

* Degree in Horticulture, plus Landscape Design training (Radcliffe College).

* Proven expertise in garden center management.

* Extensive knowledge of plant materials and all aspects of gardening.

* Additional expertise in administration and customer service.

WORK HISTORY

HORTICULTURIST
Edgestone Nursery, Inc., Burlington, MA (1990 to Present)
A full-scale nursery and garden center with a high-volume landscape division

Provide guidance to individual and corporate customers on plant care issues. Offer landscape design consultation, including preparing drawings. Advise customers on plant installation and special horticultural problems. Lead instructional seminars for groups of up to 25 on plant care and maintenance. Create sales displays. Inventory and price merchandise, process orders. Sell plants and other merchandise. Prepare special order materials.

Achievements:

● Appointed Head of Perennial and Greenhouse operations.

● Oversee all operations in the absence of the manager.

● Received outstanding performance evaluation for customer service expertise and efficiency in performing all other operations.

● Received highest performance incentive.

LANDSCAPE DESIGNER/ASSISTANT MANAGER
Knowles Company, Billerica, MA (1984 to 1988)

Provided residential landscape design services for all customers. Prepared drawings, made site visits, oversaw installations. Provided instruction to construction crews. Managed all administrative and financial functions for this $750,000/annum firm. Provided customer service.

Achievements:

● Completed all work on time and under budget.

● Designed special environment gardens, including waterfront and woodland sites.

● Received numerous letters of commendation for superior design work.

MASTER GARDENER
Minuteman National Historic Park, Concord, MA (1981 to 1984)

Created this new position to install extensive gardens. Renovated old perennial beds. Revitalized old trees and shrubs to restore grounds. Oversaw installation of new plants, shrubs, and trees.

LORRAINE T. ADAMS
Page 2

Achievements:

● Cited in regional newspaper for outstanding work.

● Commended by Iris Society of America.

● Received numerous letters from patrons and visitors praising the gardens.

● Promoted to position from Maintenance Department.

<u>PREVIOUS</u> <u>EXPERIENCE</u> includes three years at the Massachusetts Horticultural Society Bookstore in Boston, MA, as *Assistant Bookstore Manager*.

EDUCATION

<u>CERTIFICATE PROGRAM IN LANDSCAPE DESIGN</u> (1982-1984)
Radcliffe College, Cambridge, MA
Maintained 4.0 average

<u>ASSOCIATE'S DEGREE IN HORTICULTURE</u> (1981)
Mass Bay Community College, Wellesley, MA
Dean's List and Honor Roll every semester

* Received Honor Society Award, 1981
* Received Emily Seaber Parcher Award from Massachusetts Horticultural Society, 1981

NUMEROUS HORTICULTURAL SEMINARS at the Arnold Arboretum, Plant Propagation Society, Wildflower Society, etc. ACCOUNTING and MATH courses at Lowell University and Middlesex Community College.

ACTIVITIES AND INTERESTS

● Volunteer Horticulturist, Arnold Arboretum

● Chair, Red Cross Blood Drive (at Mass Bay Community College)

● Volunteer Convention Assistant, Massachusetts Horticultural Society Flower Show

Interests include gardening, hiking, making pottery, quilting, and biking.

REFERENCES

Provided upon request.

HOSPITAL ADMINISTRATOR
Sample Resume

LISA VAN ALTMAN
121 Marion Road
Burlington, Vermont
(703) 523-5767

**PROFESSIONAL
EXPERIENCE**

Administration
- Conducted statistical analyses and prepared statistical reports documenting activity and census of the hospital.
- Trained and supervised support staff.
- Advised medical staff of administrative procedures and legal considerations. Enforced adherence.
- Coordinated patient transfers with receiving facilities.
- Covered for other administrators in their absence.
- Wrote reports on interactions with outside agencies.

Management
- Assumed ultimate responsibility for night operation of a 23-building, 700 bed medical and psychiatric facility.
- Intervened in emergency situations. Invoked off-duty personnel and police intervention, when necessary.
- Conducted building inspections, safety inspections, and time studies.

Client Services
- Conducted intake interviews with patients to determine eligibility for services.
- Provided crisis counseling and advocacy.
- Coordinated services with family members and dealt with their concerns.
- Interviewed families of deceased veterans to arrange burial procedures and advise them of entitlement to V.A. assistance.

ACCOMPLISHMENTS
- AWARDED Certificate from Medical Administration Service National Training Program.
- RECEIVED Letter of Commendation from V.A. Headquarters, Washington, for ranking in top 15% of administrators.
- SELECTED from peers to initiate a program to identify insurance cases.
- KNOW QUME and WANG computer systems.

WORK HISTORY
1988-present, Night Coordinator, VA Medical Center, Burlington, VT
1986-88, Claims Clerk, VA Medical Center, Burlington, VT
1985, Medical Clerk, RGY Medical Center, Columbus, Ohio

REFERENCES
Available upon request

```
┌─────────────────────────────────────────┐
│ HUMAN SERVICES MANAGER                   │
│ Sample Resume                            │
└─────────────────────────────────────────┘
```

GORDON SAMUELS
571 Normandy Court
Indianapolis, IN 39073
(717) 922-3472

SUMMARY OF EXPERIENCE

Over six years of management experience, with specific background in the management of human
service programs.

AREAS OF EXPERTISE

Administration

- Staff recruitment, supervision, and training
- Budget management
- Knowledge of sophisticated accounting procedures
- Program planning and coordination
- Public relations
- Monitoring and evaluating programs
- Know IBM, Macintosh, and Data General computer systems

Direct Service

- Designing and implementing treatment plans
- Performing intake interviews
- Monitoring client progress
- Counseling clients; advocacy
- Crisis intervention

PROFESSIONAL EXPERIENCE

COMMUNITY HOUSE, INC., Lower Falls, Indiana

House Manager   1988 to Present

Oversee operation of this facility for severely emotionally disturbed and mildly retarded young adults.
Supervise staff of five. Provide staff training and supervision. Monitor progress of residents and
supervise implementation of treatment plans. Represent program to the community. Maintain budget.
Act as human rights officer. Write relevant reports. Attend training conferences.

BEVERLY STREET CENTER, Shelby, Indiana

Assistant Overnight Manager   1986 to 1987

Supervised three facilities housing mentally retarded adults. Performed counseling and crisis
intervention functions. Supervised three counselors.

Assistant Accounting Manager (part-time)

Processed payroll for staff of over 300. Administered bookkeeping functions, including preparing
monthly trial balance, accounts receivable, accounts payable, monthly reports. Maintained bank
accounts for 20 clients.

C.A.R.E., Inc., Indianapolis, IN

Senior Accountant (part-time)   1986 to 1987

Prepared monthly trial balance. Processed payroll. Oversaw accounts receivable and accounts payable.
Prepared statements, journals, deposits, bank reconciliations and quarterly tax returns. Verified client
income and made collection calls.

MANIONS, Watertown, MA

<u>Assistant</u> <u>Manager</u>   1984 to 1985

Managed store operations. Supervised staff of 15. Resolved customer problems. Designed displays and arranged floor set-up. Monitored inventory. Coordinated scheduling. Processed payroll.

EDUCATION

LAZAR COLLEGE, Indianapolis, IN
Certificate in Accounting, 1987

BOSTON CONSERVATORY OF MUSIC, Boston, MA
B.A. in Music/Theater, 1985
Received four-year scholarship for performance merit.
Co-chairperson of Black Student Council.

HIGH SCHOOL OF MUSIC AND ART, New York
President of senior class. Performed in MGM movie "Fame." Won Junior Achievers' Award.

ACTIVITIES and AWARDS

VOLUNTEER COUNSELOR
Youth at Risk, Indianapolis, IN, 1988 to Present.

JUDGE
Annual Sing-Off Competition, Lenox Hotel, Boston, MA, 1986.
(Won first place in contest in 1985.)

TALENT WINNER
NBC "Star of the Day" with Dave Maynard, for singing, 1986.

REFERENCES

Available upon request

MARION LEMUAL
31 Hope Street
Nashville, TN 45901
(529) 589-1694

EXHIBITIONS

- "Flour Soup" (offset book). Wood Gallery, Atlanta, 1989
- "Flour Soup," Red Eye Gallery, Nashville, TN, May, 1988
- 16mm Film, Junior Film Show, Studio Gallery, Evansville, IN, June, 1988
- Color Photographs, Group Show, Wood Gallery, 1987
- Black and White Photographs, Nashville, TN, May, 1986

PROFESSIONAL EXPERIENCE

ILLUSTRATOR/DESIGNER, **The Finer Company,** Clark River, TN
A division of Sherle Wagner, Atlanta, GA   1989

Design of exhibition quality bathroom furniture and tiles. Illustrate catalogs and promotional materials.
Photograph model setups.

FREELANCE ILLUSTRATOR/DESIGNER
                                                                            1982 to Present
Produce illustrations for corporate promotions including pen and ink drawings and photographs. Design
posters, corporate catalogs, brochures, fliers, logos and signs. Create unique environments for store
interiors using three-dimensional design. Do photographic portraiture.

Recent clients include:
- Bates Shoe Company, Nashville, TN
- Passport Clothing, Nashville, TN
- Dorr and Scheff, Dicson, TN
- Berk's Shoe Store, Clarkson, TN

PRODUCTION ASSISTANT, Hellotrope Studies, Nashville, TN
                                                                            1987 to 1988
Begin as intern and was asked to continue on at end of internship. Assisted with all aspects of shoots
including lighting, sets, electricity, loading cameras. Oversaw dubbing. Maintained film library. Set up
computerized mailing lists. Provided administrative support.

PRODUCTION/RESEARCH ASSISTANT, The "Break Time" Film Project
                                                                            1988 to Present
Undertake pre-production work for narrative film including grant and funding research, solicitation of
funds, and public relations.

TEACHING ASSISTANT, R.I.S.D., Providence, Rhode Island
                                                                            2/88 to 6/88
Selected by faculty for this position. Taught operation and maintenance of offset press, plate maker,
hand press, stat camera. Scheduled and supervised student use of equipment. Graded student work.
Maintained studio, equipment and stockroom. Printed R.I.S.D.'s first 4-color comic book.

MARION LEMUAL   **Page 2**

EQUIPMENT EXPERTISE

- STILL CAMERAS: 35mm, 2 1/4, 4x5 and 8x10 format.
- MOVIE CAMERAS: Super 8mm, 16mm (Bolex and CP 130).
- DARKROOM: Black and white and color developing and printing processes including Hope and Col-enta processors and the Cibachrome process.
- OFFSET REPRODUCTION: A.B. Dick 360 offset press, 20x24 hand press.
- SOUND EQUIPMENT: Nagra 8mm sound recorder.
- COMPUTER EQUIPMENT: Apple Macintosh.

EDUCATION

RHODE ISLAND SCHOOL OF DESIGN, Providence, Rhode Island
B.F.A. in Photography; Minor in Film   1984 to 1988
Graduated cum laude.
Projects included: "Flour Soup" (pictorial family history using offset printing); 16mm fictional and documentary films; three still photography exhibits.

REFERENCES AND PORTFOLIO

Available upon request

INDUSTRIAL/MECHANICAL
DESIGNER
Sample Resume

LAURENCE S. FIBKINS
3544 Altemere Turnpike, Bellevue, WA 61842   (526) 669-8032

DESIGNER
Optical/Electro-Optical/Industrial

SUMMARY: Versatile designer with extensive background in mechanical, optical, electro-optical, and industrial design.

EXPERTISE:
- Electro-optical systems (ground, airborne, satellite instrument systems; test equipment; telescopes; optical trackers, sighting systems).
- Medical instruments (blood analysis, radiation, surgical, optical examination).
- Vehicle design (survivability design; off-road and military vehicles).
- Heavy industrial equipment (sheet metal enclosures, ducting, radiation shielding, support structures).
- Miscellaneous: Aircraft altimeters, spectrograph components, solar powered kilns, aerospace and defense support equipment, airborne gun and ammo-handling systems).

PROFESSIONAL EXPERIENCE:

Mechanical Designer (contract)
Intrametrics/Degnin, Seattle, WA (1990)

Designed military and commercial infrared imaging scanners, telescopes, controls, and accessories (multi-use carts, man-portable equipment).

Senior Designer (1983 to 1989)
Lanmann Instrument Company, Bellevue, WA

Design barometric aircraft altimeters and airspeed indicators; tank optical sighting systems; and tooling for manufacturing of electro-optical instruments. Provide documentation of test equipment. Act as group leader. Contact vendors. Monitor costs. Coordinate with optical engineering, photographic, publications, manufacturing, and quality control departments.

Designer (1974 to 1983)
Contract positions with the following companies:

RCA, Government Systems Div., Tacoma, WA (1983)
Designed trailer-mounted racks for military black boxes.

Northwest Research Center, Seattle, WA (1983)
Designed precision micro-positioning devices for electronic sensors.

UWS Labs, Inc., Bellevue, WA (1982)
Designed optical components and structures for high-energy laser system.

Instrumentation Lab, Monroe, WA (1982)
Designed packaging of electronic components for clinical diagnostic system and layouts of new optical detector.

Electronic Imaging, Seattle, WA (1980-81)
Designed radar structures.

Space Research Corp, North Troy, VT (1979)
Designed tractor/cab section of military/industrial vehicles. Determined human factor requirement for seating, visibility, survival.

LAURENCE S. FIBKINS
Page 2

Union Carbide, Albany, NY (1977-78)
Designed radiation shielding for medical devices. Designed automatic pipettor, reagent pumps, incubator separators.

Electrolux Corp., Rochester, NY (1976)
Designed new vacuum cleaners, especially housings and controls. Involved injection molding, metal stamping.

Allistair-Jenks, Danbury, CT (1975-76)
Designed optical assemblies, mechanisms, and structures for NASA Large Space Telescope guidance system.

Anro Labs, Columbia University, NY (1975)
Designed radiation shield to protect personnel working with radioactive materials in a 60-foot cyclotron.

Mechanical Designer (1973-74)
Teradyne Corp., Stamford, CT

Designed new line of modular electrostatic paint-spray booths; plant layouts for installation of painting systems.

Electromechanical Designer (1972-73)
National Instrument Makers, Inc., White Plains, NY

Designed electrostatic surgical operating instruments. Coordinated work of prototype lab and design/drafting group. Also designed camera/borescope adapters and developed improved lung forceps.

EDUCATION: *University of Bridgeport*, Bridgeport, CT
Bachelor of Science in Industrial Design

ADDITIONAL COURSES in math, German, personnel management, educational and industrial psychology at the University of Connecticut and the University of Bridgeport.

AWARDS: NASA Commendation for work on Infrared Horizon Scanners

Kollsman Commendation (team) for work on Electro-Optical Sighting Devices.

ACTIVITIES: Past President, Fairfield County Astronomical Society.

Member, American Ordnance Society, Greenpeace, Planetary Society.

Interests include amateur astronomy, photography, environmental preservation, motor vehicles.

REFERENCES: Provided upon request.

ALLISON ADORNO
56 Leonard Court
Nashua, New Hampshire 51403
(603) 598-9832

SUMMARY

Strong background representing needs of both clients and company; extensive research experience; proven ability to provide counsel to distressed clients.

PROFESSIONAL EXPERTISE

- Performing extensive research to establish client liability; reviewing official documents and reports, interviewing physicians, attorneys and other professionals; analyzing data.

- Interviewing clients in crisis situations; answering questions, advising on options, providing intervention and support.

- Negotiating between company and client; balancing company's interests with client's rights and needs.

- Writing professional reports and correspondence; designing logos and other promotional materials.

- Know CRT, Macintosh, and IBM computer systems and software.

WORK HISTORY

NORTHEAST PROPERTY AND LIABILITY INSURANCE COMPANY, Nashua, NH
Casualty Claims Adjuster (1989 to Present)
Negotiate and settle personal injury and property damage claims for caseload of over 100 clients. Verify client coverage and fill out claims on-line.

- Interview clients to determine details of accident, medical coverage, and follow-up undertaken by client.

- Answer clients' questions regarding company policies, benefits, restrictions, and procedures.

- Conduct extensive research with third parties -- including attorneys, physicians, witnesses, and other insurance companies -- to establish liability.

- Evaluate medical reports to screen for pre-existing conditions and to determine what role accident played in reported condition.

- Settle property damage claims with attorneys and third-party clients.

- Make liability determinations using taped reports, police reports, and collateral materials.

UNIVERSAL LABORATORIES, Nashua, NH (1985-89/Part-Time)
Administrative Assistant
Managed office for this manufacturing firm. Oversaw financial operations, including payroll, cash disbursements, and receivables. Screened job applicants. Established information tracking systems.

THE CORNER FITNESS CENTER, Keene, NH (1989/Part-Time)
Marketing/Customer Service Assistant
Produced promotional materials for this organization. Designed original logo; oversaw application of logo to marketable clothing, brochures, and fliers. Developed relations with printer. Enrolled new members; provided customer services to current members.

EDUCATION

KEENE STATE COLLEGE, Keene, New Hampshire
Bachelor of Science in Business Management/Communications, 1989
Numerous courses in Communications, Marketing, Human Resources, and Business Management.

References provided upon request.

ARNOLD H. LENMAN
495 Walnut Street
Portland, Maine 67962
(619) 340-2354

SUMMARY

Highly skilled **LANDSCAPE SUPERVISOR** with considerable additional background in administration and marketing.

PROFESSIONAL EXPERTISE

Project Management

- Proven ability to complete complex and demanding projects with small crews and limited equipment.
- Track record achieving exceptional profit margins, completing all jobs on time and under-budget, leaving no "loose ends."
- Outstanding record in developing new accounts, increasing business by up to 70%.
- Maintain exceptionally high level of morale among staff, and sustain superior relations with architects.
- Considerable experience assuming complete management responsibility for all aspects of a landscape business, overseeing multiple projects and supervising up to 30 workers.

Technical Skills

Equipment: Know Bobcat Loader, Hydroseeder, Backhoe, Tractor with Rock Rakes, 3-Yard Loader. Have Class 1 driving permit.

Horticultural Knowledge: Vast knowledge of plant identification. Oversee sensitive transplants of trees and shrubs. Extensive knowledge of plant care and maintenance.

Masonry/Carpentry: High-level masonry work including chimneys, fireplaces, stonework, brickwork, concrete unit pavers, bluestone, granite. Carpentry skills include decks, fencing, arbors, and trellises.

WORK HISTORY

T. MILLMAN & COMPANY, Portland, ME (1990 to Present)
Landscape Foreman

Supervise work crews of up to 30. Hire and supervise subcontractors. Meet with architects to discuss specifications and set site visit schedules. Set construction schedules. Arrange logistics for material deliveries. Train and evaluate staff. Oversee progress of project. Produce hands-on landscape, masonry, and carpentry work.

Accomplishments:

- Completed all jobs on time and under budget.
- Installed large trees weighing up to six tons (10" caliper).
- Completed residential jobs ranging from $40,000 to $150,000, achieving exceptional profit margins.
- Selected by major outside firm as "designated foreman." Company would only accept bids from T. Millman contingent on my participation as foreman.
- Maintained exceptionally high level of staff morale, with the most in-demand work crews.

EARTHWORKS/MATTESON, Yarmouth, ME
Project Manager/Sales/Estimator (1986-89)
Promoted from position in design/sales.

Acted as General Manager for company's Landscape Division, overseeing 21 employees. Marketed services to commercial customers. Wrote direct mail materials, oversaw telemarketing, offered bids using Dodge Reports listings. Tracked finances and ensured maintenance of profitability. Scheduled, supervised, and implemented up to four projects at a time. Hired all staff, conducting national searches when necessary. Participated in development of computer estimating program. Located vendors and oversaw buying for Landscape Division. Acted as technical expert to developers on erosion control problems.

Accomplishments:

● Increased volume of commercial accounts by 70%.

● Sold $700,000 of work in first year.

● Developed, coordinated, and marketed hydroseed program that led to 40% profit margins.

● Selected to attend International Conference on Erosion Control (New Orleans, 1988), and Charles Vander Kois Estimating Seminar.

THE LENMAN COMPANY, Brunswick, Maine
Owner (1982-86)

Built this quality-oriented landscape business from the ground floor to $750,000 in annual sales. Supervised commercial and high-end residential projects. Established working relationships with prominent landscape architects. Completed hydroseeding projects. Supervised 12 staff and oversaw all operations.

TERRASOL INC., Boston, MA
Production Supervisor/Project Manager (1978-82)

Coordinated complex projects including **The Arsenal Mall** in Watertown, MA and **Analogic Corporation** in Peabody. Scheduled crews and assigned job orders to foreman. Managed operations facility in Tewksbury, MA, overseeing maintenance and distribution of all equipment and plant materials. Visited job sites and reviewed progress with foremen. Consolidated daily job reports and tracked job progress according to bid. Hired employees.

EDUCATION

WENTWORTH INSTITUTE OF TECHNOLOGY, Boston, MA
● **Received Certificate in Construction Management,** 1981
● **Received Certificate in Surveying**, 1981
Achieved superior evaluations.

CHARLES VANDER KOIS ESTIMATING SEMINAR, Washington, D.C. (1988)

INTERNATIONAL EROSION CONTROL SEMINAR, New Orleans, LA (1988)

INTERESTS

Small-scale farming, bicycling, boating, cross-country skiing.

References available upon request.

LAWYER
Sample Resume

PATRICIA W. BECKER
Box 51
Bernallilo, New Mexico 54533
(903) 430-4326

BACKGROUND   Broad-based legal professional with successful background in law and legal affairs, management, labor and employee relations, lobbying, and regulatory compliance. Litigation experience includes divorce, criminal, and real estate cases.

EXPERIENCE

**Law and Legal
Affairs**

As *private practice attorney,* handled a wide range of cases including matrimonial, real estate, wills, probate, and criminal proceedings.

Provided legal services for sexually abused children. Extensive practice in Family Court including custody, support, abuse, neglect, and juvenile delinquency cases.

Advised university president on legal issues such as student rights, liability, and risk management. Investigated allegations of negligence brought against college.

**Lobbying and
Legislative
Affairs**

As a *legislative representative,* drafted and reviewed legislation relating to education and labor relations issues. Advocated positions on bills pending in the legislature.

Conducted seminars and workshops regarding legislation and lobbying.

Drafted and successfully lobbied four-year payment plan focused on reducing 60% increase in state health insurance premiums affecting school districts.

**Labor Relations
and Affirmative
Action**

As *Assistant to University President,* offered advice on employee relations, labor contract compliance, affirmative action, and sexual harassment.

Acted as President's designee in all labor management matters, and as hearing officer for all union grievances on campus.

Organized retrenchment plan for 30 teaching positions in compliance with labor contracts.

Responsible for all Affirmative Action compliance, and articulation of college policy.

Drafted a bill designed to create greater professional accountability for teachers.

**Teaching and
Training**

As *Adjunct Professor,* taught undergraduate law courses in the Political Science Department and Education Law courses in the Educational Administration Department.

Developed unique training program designed to educate and advance legal assistants to position of paralegal. Programs promoted more efficient operations.

Management

As *Assistant to University President,* acted as a member of the executive management team.

Managed a law office, including recruiting, hiring, training, and evaluating both staff attorneys and legal assistants.

Managed the opening of new law offices.

PATRICIA W. BECKER
Page 2

EMPLOYMENT HISTORY

1989-Current	<u>Special Agent,</u> Southwestern Mutual Life Insurance Company, Albuquerque, NM
1986-1988	<u>Legislative Representative</u>, New Mexico State School Boards Association, Santa Fe, New Mexico
1981-1986	<u>Private Law Practice:</u> *Managing Attorney,* Desmond Legal Services, Santa Fe, NM *Associate,* John W. Ryalski, Albuquerque, NM *Private practice,* Albuquerque, NM
1979-1985	State University of New Mexico, Albuquerque, NM <u>Adjunct Professor in Political Science and Educational Administration</u> (1984-85) <u>Assistant to the President for Legal Affairs, Employee Relations, and Affirmative Action</u>
1978-1979	<u>Associate</u>, Norman Doblin, Esq., Roswell, NM

EDUCATION

1978, J.D., Western New England College, Springfield, MA

1974, M.S. in Education, State University of New York at Oswego, Oswego, NY

1971, B.S., William Smith College, Geneva, NY

```
MARKETING
REPRESENTATIVE
Sample Resume
```

SUZANNE DAYMAN
73 Stillwell Road
San Diego, CA 46944
(238) 626-8901

HIGHLIGHTS

- Increased revenues at Dayman & Company from zero to over $4 million in three years.

- Proven ability to integrate customer service and sales functions, resulting in greatly increased productivity and profitability.

- Consistently excelled in all marketing and sales endeavors, building a loyal customer base and winning numerous awards.

WORK HISTORY

DAYMAN & COMPANY, San Diego, CA (1986 to Present)
Wholesalers of Womens' Clothing
Independent Representative

Built this highly successful sales organization from the ground floor, representing major manufacturers to retail outlets throughout the Northwest. Established and maintain over 300 active retail accounts, including large chains, department stores, and small specialty stores. Supervise a staff of four, providing full sales and customer service training. Coordinate all sales presentations and manage major accounts. Implemented an order-tracking and customer service system, increasing company profits by 15-20% annually. Design marketing materials and organize trade shows. Provide outside consultation to clients on sales techniques, merchandising, and financial management.

Accomplishments:

- Substantially increased revenues for all manufacturers represented:
- Increased Gym Tonic Sportswear from $100,000 to $1.5 million in less than a year, making Southern California their highest revenue territory.
- Doubled sales for Jennifer Reed Sweaters (from $900,000 to over $2 million).
- Won awards from Christina Swimwear and Gym Tonic for being the Number One rep nationally.
- Built exceptionally loyal customer base, receiving numerous requests from manufacturers to represent them.

L.W. BRENTANO, San Diego, CA (1985 to 1986)
Manufacturer of Womens' Clothing
Showroom Manager

Responsible for management of regional corporate showroom. Identified target markets; designed and mailed promotional materials to prospective accounts. Generated new clients through direct marketing, increasing sales substantially. Established an account base of well over 200 stores, many of which are active. Initiated a sales tracking system that is still in use. Coordinated regional trade shows including developing promotions, designing displays, scheduling sales presentations, and merchandising.

SUZANNE DAYMAN
Page 2

Accomplishments:

- Brought in well over $1 million in new business in first year.
- Increased volume with existing accounts by 50%.
- Received substantial bonuses and commission raises due to superb performance.

XEROX CORPORATION, San Francisco, CA (1982 to 1985)

Sales Trainee (1985)
Participated in training seminars and classes to learn the fundamentals of sales. Gained extensive knowledge of Xerox equipment, pricing, policies. Handled sales calls and on-site demonstrations with sales representatives and managers. Completed independent study of various sales tapes and manuals.

Accomplishments:

- Chosen to participate in Management Training (out of pool of 40).
- Promoted twice in two years to this position.

Customer Service Representative (1983-1984)
Resolved supply, service, and billing issues for all major and Level II accounts. Gave presentations to sales teams and traveled with reps to promote better customer relations. Responsible for all aspects of customer service for assigned sales teams.

Accomplishments:

- Won awards every quarter for successful intervention in sales team problems.
- Received numerous letters of commendation for resolving difficult problems that had been stumping predecessors for years.
- Selected to be member of four-person team to pilot a new customer service system for Xerox International.
- Promoted from position as receptionist (1982).

EDUCATION

BERKELEY UNIVERSITY, Berkeley, CA (1982-85)
Major in Marketing and Management

NUMEROUS PROFESSIONAL DEVELOPMENT SEMINARS, including "Leadership Through Quality," "Employee Involvement," "Management Skills Training."

SPECIAL INTERESTS

Volunteer Supervisor at the Boy's and Girl's Club of Oceanside, CA

Member, National Association of Female Executives

Activities include tennis, skiing, and mountain biking.

MECHANICAL TECHNICIAN
Sample One-Page Resume

ALEX DEVEREAUX
11 Woodlawn Court
Bethpage, NY 10036
(516)645-5612

SKILLS SUMMARY
- Drafting and interpreting blueprints
- Arc, TIG, and MIG welding
- Fabricating custom parts; building and modifying engines
- Strong writing and business management skills

PROFESSIONAL EXPERIENCE

TERASOL, INC., New Hyde Park, NY
Mechanical Technician   1988 to Present
- Produce and test 200kw and 30kw cogeneration units.
- Oversee related research and development efforts.
- Design engine modifications.
- Interpret blueprints for co-workers.

LEVITTOWN MOTORS, Levittown, NY
Jaguar Technician   1986 to 1988
- Handled all phases of auto repair.
- Installed accessories.
- Oversaw electro-mechanical troubleshooting.

TOMMY'S AUTO REPAIR, Pelham, NY
Mechanical Technician   1984 to 1986
- Delivered general auto repairs.

ANDOVER DEVICES, Flushing, NY
Technician   1982 to 1984
- Handled all phases of electro-mechanical work to produce computer test systems.
- Drafted new designs and engineering change orders.
- Assumed responsibility for all testing, modifications, and quality of systems.

EDUCATION

NASSAU COMMUNITY COLLEGE, Bethpage, NY
Major courses: Business Administration, Electrical Engineering.

INTERESTS

Playing percussion, mountain biking, skiing, personal development.

REFERENCES

Available upon request

| NURSE/ADMINISTRATOR |
| Sample Resume |

ADRIENNE FOX
427-A Sand Hill Road
Columbus, Ohio 59032
(607) 571-6754

SUMMARY

Health care administrator with clinical expertise (R.N.) and significant background in program development, staff supervision and training, clinic management, and direct care.

PROFESSIONAL EXPERIENCE

1985-Present

CENTRAL COMMUNITY HEALTH PLAN
Columbus Health Center, Columbus, OH

Instrumental in starting this new clinic. Worked with a core team of 15 managers to develop clinic practices and structure. Supervised up to three departments (Visual Services, Medical Specialties, and Surgical Specialties) with 20 clinical and 6 clerical staff. Oversee day-to-day department operations, provide clinical information to non-clinical administrators, supervise clinician productivity, provide patient advocacy and troubleshooting when necessary, and execute strategic planning.

Accomplishments:
*   Developed patient flow systems, organizational charts, personnel practices, record-keeping forms, inventory systems, vendor contacts, etc.

*   Hired all clinical, technical, and clerical staff for three departments.

*   Initiated innovative staff training plan. Arranged visits to local hospitals and clinics to view surgeries and diagnostic testing procedures, and established a cross-training program (staff members learn each others' jobs).

*   Wrote Department Manuals documenting systems and practices for each department. Won Department of Public Health approval.

*   Wrote Orientation Manuals for clinical staff.

*   Act as Chief Coordinator of community Blood Pressure Clinic.

*   Created patient education program. Wrote instructional pamphlets.

*   Received Key Contribution Award, 1988, 1986

Danforth Health Center, Urbana, OH (1985-87)
Coordinated practice of seven surgeons. Prepared sessions, offered direct patient care, directed patient flow system, acted as patient advocate, triaged phone calls, offered patient education, ordered supplies. Was Code Team member and resource clinician for staff.
Created own position from temporary position.

1981-1985

OHIO VALLEY MEDICAL CENTER, Springfield, Ohio
Registered Nurse, Charge Nurse

Offered nursing services to patients. Acted as Chairperson of the Documentation Committee, where introduced improved charting procedures and facilitated communication among all health personnel. Appointed to Advisory Committee under Ohio State Board of Nursing to review Ohio Nurse Practice Act. Served as Ostomy resource person; offered inservice workshops on care of ostomy patients.

ADRIENNE FOX
Page 2

1978-1979   UNIVERSITY HEALTH SERVICES, UNIVERSITY OF OHIO
Columbus, OH

Played a key role in the development of the first womens' health care program at the University.

EDUCATION

1985   Masters Program in Public Health
Loma Linda University, California (Off-Campus Program)

1979-1981   Springfield Hospital School of Nursing, Springfield, OH
R.N., 1981

1976-1979   University of Chicago, Chicago, Illinois
B.A. in Physical Anthropology, 1979
Minor: Nutrition

ADDITIONAL TRAINING includes numerous courses in supervision and clinical issues at Danforth Community Health Plan, Chemistry at Ohio State; and Nursing Seminars including PMS Update, Aids Update, etc.,

LICENSURE AND
CERTIFICATION   R.N. Ohio License #173035; Michigan License #64774
BCLS Certification.

ORGANIZATIONS   Ohio Nurses' Association
American Nurses' Association

ACTIVITIES   Songwriting, flying (co-pilot single engine plane), skiing, acting.

REFERENCES   Available upon request.

> **PASTOR**
> Sample Resume

MARGO ANDERSON
98 Riverside Drive, Battle Creek, MI 52673   (617) 862-3572

SUMMARY

Committed Pastor with proven leadership abilities, clinical counseling credentials, administrative skills, and church experience. Seeking a church position with emphasis on fostering and maintaining Christian community.

PROFESSIONAL EXPERIENCE

Church Experience   *1984 - Present*

World Council of Churches Conference on Mission and Evangelism, Special Delegate, San Antonio, TX.

- One of seven delegates representing Renford Theology School at this world-wide conference of all faiths.
- Led forum to share experience with other seminarians.
- Organized network consisting of members of the various faiths represented.

Supply Preaching, United Methodist Church, Marshall, MI

Member, Outreach Committee, Pilgrim Church, Kalamazoo, MI

- Coordinated letter writing program for Amnesty International.

Church Council Member (elected to position), Pilgrim Church, Kalamazoo, MI

- Initiated, organized and led adult discussion group focussed on spiritual issues which meets twice weekly and has a regular membership of 10 - 15. Group has run continuously since 1985.
- Served as Chairperson of Educational Ministries. Oversaw Adult Education and Sunday School. Coordinated teachers and parents.
- Served communion.
- Made visitation calls with special focus on the elderly.

Chaplain Intern, Sancta Maria Hospital, Battle Creek, MI
(Clinical Pastoral Education).

- Visited patients in the hospital. Provided variety of services including prayer, advocacy and ministering to families of patients.
- Led worship service.
- Participated in team ministry.

Minister Intern, Rand UCC Church, Grand Rapids, MI

- Participated in team ministry.
- Preached.
- Made visitation calls with special focus on the elderly.
- Acted as resource and consultant to Sunday School teachers.

Psychotherapy Experience   *1973 - 1987*

<u>Psychotherapist,</u> Marshall Psychiatric Counseling Association, Marshall, MI (A private group practice).

- Provided long-term psychotherapy and crisis intervention for adults, children and families.
- Served as resource and consultant to teachers, principals, guidance counselors and probation officers.
- Participated in case management teams.
- Presented case materials at clinical staff meetings.

<u>Staff Social Worker,</u> Kalamazoo Youth Guidance Center, Kalamazoo, MI

- Provided family therapy, crisis intervention and referral services.
- Supervised case-aids and interns.
- Provided Parent Effectiveness Training.
- Served as resource and consultant to teachers, principals, guidance counselors and probation officers.
- Participated in case management teams.
- Presented case materials at clinical staff meetings.

EDUCATION

<u>Renford Theology School,</u> Grand Rapids, MI
Master of Divinity, 1989

<u>University of Arizona School of Social Work,</u> Tempe, AZ
M.S.W., 1973

<u>University of Arizona,</u> Tempe, AZ
B.S. in Human Development , 1969

OTHER CREDENTIALS

Licensed Independent Clinical Social Worker, 1982 - Present.

Smith College School of Social Work, Summer Institute, 1980.

Certified Instructor in Parent Effectiveness Training (PET) and Teacher Effectiveness Training (TET), 1973.
- Taught eight PET courses and one TET course.

Devine Hospital Institute for Special Needs Children, 1972.
- Certificate granted.

INTERESTS AND ACTIVITIES

- UCC Trustee, Star Island Corporation Board
  (Star Island is an educational and religious retreat).
- Parent Volunteer, Citizen's Advisory Committee, Kalamazoo Public Schools.

```
PERSONNEL OFFICER
(Military)
Sample Resume
```

MICHAEL R. DAVIDSON
425 Oak Tree Avenue
Gatonia, North Carolina 45888
(517) 709-1065

BACKGROUND

Management

- **Administered all personnel actions** for a 669-member unit.

- **Managed all administrative and clerical operations for a 669-member unit,** including administering payroll, allocating awards, producing and writing efficiency reports, and overseeing staff.

- **Oversaw administration of $6-million worth of equipment,** including procurement and resource allocation.

- **Wrote 75-page procedural manual** and numerous official reports for the Army.

- **Know Multimate** and Word Processing programs.

- **Received numerous awards** and commendations for outstanding performance.

- **Received Management degree from West Point;** graduated within top third of major.

Staff Supervision and Training

- **Provided direct supervision for a 61-member unit,** including all aspects of training, assessment, coaching, and discipline.

- **Delivered classroom training** and field training.

- **Designed courses;** assigned and trained instructors; chose course materials.

- **Assessed performance** of all staff members (written and verbal reviews).

- **Identified problems** of staff members (such as substance abuse and personal crises) and referred for counseling.

WORK HISTORY

PERSONNEL ADMINISTRATION OFFICER (1989-90)
United States Army, Camp Davay, Philippines
Managed a 10-member team that administered all personnel actions for a 572-member battalion plus 97 civilian employees.

- Handled all financial matters, including processing payroll.
- Supervised line managers.
- Acted as special assistant to the Colonel.
- Oversaw clerical operations, directed work flow, developed and managed administrative systems.
- Directed enforcement of military justice; arranged legal counsel for defendants and counseled defendants of rights.
- Wrote and produced reports and materials.

BATTALION LIAISON OFFICER (1989)
United States Army, Camp Davay, Philippines
Planned and directed all operations for a 572-member battalion. Evaluated staff training needs and implemented training programs. Made decisions about resource allocation and procured equipment. Assessed performance of units and reviewed training efficacy. Supervised and evaluated line officers.

ADDITIONAL POSITIONS WITH THE U.S. ARMY:
- *Fire Support Officer* (1987-89), Fort Lim, Texas
- *Executive Officer* (1986-87), Fort Lim, Texas
- *Fire Direction Officer* (1985-86), Fort Lim, Texas

MICHAEL R. DAVIDSON
Page 2

ACHIEVEMENTS

<u>Rated "Best Officer in the Battalion"</u> in every position held.

<u>Increased rating of unit</u> for efficiency and overall performance from bottom third of 106 units to third place, Department of the Army ratings.

<u>Received two Army Commendation Medals</u> for exceptionally meritorious service (1989, 1990).

<u>Received four Army Achievement Medals</u> for outstanding performance (1985, 1986, 1989).

<u>Received Saint Barbara's Award</u> (1987). Given to the top Field Artillery Officer in a battalion for displayed technical competence.

<u>Nominee for the General Douglas MacArthur Leadership Award</u> on basis of "duty, honor, and country."

<u>Promoted from Second Lieutenant</u> to First Lieutenant, 1986. Promoted to Captain, 1990.

<u>Commended by Army Committee of Excellence</u> for "providing top quality of life" for unit members.

<u>Administered Combined Federal Campaign</u> for four years (raised money for charity organizations).

<u>Have Top Secret Clearance.</u>

EDUCATION

WEST POINT ACADEMY, West Point, New York
<u>Bachelor of Science in Engineering Management,</u> 1985
Graduated within top third of major; Dean's List three semesters.

- Courses included Financial Management, Personnel Resources, Operations Research, Leadership.
- GMAT Score: 690
- Played Varsity Hockey and Handball, 1981-85.

REFERENCES

Provided upon request.

POLICE OFFICER
Sample Resume

ROGER ALIANO
6 Farrell Court
Rumford, Rhode Island 64851
I.D. # 1770
(809) 550-5983

HIGHLIGHTS

● Proven track record overseeing all aspects of security for diplomats, government officials, and chief executives of the United States and other countries.

● Extensive knowledge of roadways, hospitals, police departments, fire departments, and community facilities throughout Rhode Island.

● Graduated <u>first</u> in <u>class</u> in physical training and <u>seventh</u> in <u>class</u> in academics from the Rhode Island State Police Academy, 1982. Also, honors graduate in Criminal Justice from Providence Community College. Made Dean's List all semesters.

● Extensive experience in all aspects of police work, including security, crowd control, riot control, rescue operations, and major crime investigation.

● Received numerous Letters of Commendation from the public for service provided in emergency situations.

WORK HISTORY

<u>**RHODE ISLAND STATE POLICE**</u> (1982 to Present)
Department of Public Safety, Providence, RI
Trooper

Held a variety of assignments with units throughout Rhode Island, including:

<u>**47 Team, Troop A,**</u> Providence (1988-Present and 1985-86)
Major responsibilities include:

SECURITY
Provide security for visiting public figures including President Bush, King Hussein, the Premier of Canada, and numerous governors.
● Provide personal protection
● Escort motorcades
● Drive diplomats
● Conduct background checks on personnel
● Block roadways and other areas of access

MAJOR DISASTER/DISTURBANCE INTERVENTION
Member of six-person mobile unit that provides on-site support for major disasters and disturbances throughout Rhode Island.
● Conduct rescue operations in major disasters
● Provide riot control/crowd control
● Provide prison riot control
● Back up local police as needed

PUBLIC RELATIONS
● Provide honor guard at funerals of dignitaries
● Escort government officials at public appearances
● Participate in parades and other public relations events

ROGER ALIANO
Page 2

_____

Major Crime Bureau of Investigative Services, Providence, RI

Investigated major crimes such as murder, homicide, rape, and white collar crimes in Providence, Rumford, Bristol, and surrounding areas.
• Interviewed witnesses
• Seized evidence
• Served Governor's warrants
• Presented cases to District Attorney for prosecution.

State Police Barracks, Providence, Newport, Dover
• Patrol highways
• Investigate accidents to determine liability
• Make drunk driving arrests and warrant arrests
• Prepare written reports to use in court for prosecution
• Testify in court
• Provide desk coverage: receive calls and dispatch cruisers

EDUCATION

ASSOCIATE'S DEGREE IN CRIMINAL JUSTICE, 1982
Providence Community College, Providence, RI
Graduated with honors. Dean's List all semesters.

RHODE ISLAND STATE POLICE ACADEMY, 1982
Graduated with 99.7 average in physical training, first in class.
89.7 average in academics, seventh in class.

RUMFORD HIGH SCHOOL. Graduated 1979.
Played varsity football, hockey, and lacrosse.

SPECIAL QUALIFICATIONS

• CPR first-responder trained.

• Certified in 9mm handgun and shotgun use.

• Completed annual training update on laws and procedures.

• Background in weight training.

REFERENCES

Available upon request.

LEONA ESKAFAR
296 Abbott Street
Evanston, Illinois 62678
(681) 341-5445

OBJECTIVE: Position as a <u>COBOL</u> <u>Business</u> <u>Applications</u> <u>Programmer</u> with opportunity for advancement.

SOFTWARE: COBOL, OS JCL, FORTRAN, PL/1, VAX/VMS, DCL, DEC FMS, DEC SMG, MS/DOS, DECnet, DOS.

HARDWARE: IBM 370/4341, OS/VS1, CMS, VAX 11/780, IBM PC/AT.

EDUCATION: COMPUTER LEARNING CENTER OF CHICAGO, Evanston, IL
<u>Certificate in Computer Programming,</u> September 1989

Experience includes: coding, debugging and documenting applications programs, using Structured programming techniques, Sequential Update, Program Maintenance, Data Validation, Table Processing, Internal COBOL Sort, Multi-level control breaks, VSAM applications.

LENINGRAD STATE UNIVERSITY, USSR
<u>M.S. in Applied Mathematics,</u> 1967

EXPERIENCE: **COMPUTYPE CORPORATION**, Chicago, IL
<u>Software Engineer,</u> Type Division (1984 to Present)

Designed and developed the Compugraphic Typeface Database containing bitmap and contour data from Compugraphic's typeface library. Implemented a quality control software package to check the quality of CG's type products by graphically representing CG characters on a Vector Automation Graphicus-80 terminal and on the HP Pen Plotter. Designed, coded, debugged and tested new software; fixed problems in released software; wrote user procedures and training materials for manufacturing.

RAND-TECH, Evanston, IL
<u>Software Engineer,</u> Systems Development (1982 to 1984)

Designed and implemented graphics library routines for various application software packages. Analyzed user-interface graphic commands. Oversaw coding, debugging, and testing of new programs and provided ongoing graphics system support.

HONEYWELL, Chicago, IL
<u>Programmer/Analyst</u> (1979 to 1982)

Designed and implemented numerical and statistical routines for FORTRAN application library. Managed ongoing FORTRAN language system support for Honeywell Level-6 minicomputers.

PERSONAL: U.S. Citizen

REFERENCES: Available upon request.

> **RECREATIONAL LEADERSHIP**
> Sample Resume

ROLAND ALBRECHT
198 Robin Court
Greenwich, CT 39021
(203) 655-6890

JOB OBJECTIVE

A position in recreational leadership utilizing my background as a counselor and coordinator of programs for children.

HIGHLIGHTS

- Substantial experience planning and organizing athletic and recreational activities for elementary-aged children.
- Experience working with special needs children.
- Ability to work with diverse populations, including children, parents, and professionals.
- Program planning and development expertise.
- Successful coach. Little League Team has been in the playoffs every year since 1984. Won championship, 1986.
- Experience supervising and training staff.
- Producer, WMUC Radio Station, University of Connecticut.

EDUCATION

UNIVERSITY OF CONNECTICUT, Storrs, Connecticut
Bachelor of Arts in Communications, 1988
- Made Dean's List, 1988
- Certification in Elementary Education pending.
- Courses in child psychology, coaching, and business.

EXPERIENCE

1985 to Present

FOREST GROVE DAY CAMP, Greenwich, CT

Program Coordinator (1988)
Administer the recreational program in this camp for special needs children ages 7 to 15. Make all arrangements for camp trips, including planning, scheduling, and researching locations. Supervise program of non-competitive athletic events. Organize staff activity program in the camp for 44 counselors. Schedule athletic events with other camps. Assist in pre-camp set-up of rooms and facilities. Help with recruitment efforts.

Head Counselor (1987 - Present)
Supervise group of 18 campers (ages 10-12). Design schedule of activities and organize sports events. Offer guidance and support to campers. Provide disciplinary measures when necessary. Maintain contact with parents. Supervise staff. Act as liaison to medical professionals.

Counselor (1985-86)
Counseled a unit of special needs campers ages 12 to 14.

1987

ST. ANDREWS SCHOOL, Afterschool Program, Norwalk, CT
Teacher's Aide (Part-time)
Helped organize a program of activities for 20 children, grades K-6. Provided tutoring and homework assistance. Selected books and conducted storytime. Supervised games and sports activities.

ROLAND ALBRECHT   **Page 2**

1984 to Present	LITTLE LEAGUE BASEBALL, Greenwich, CT

1984 to Present   LITTLE LEAGUE BASEBALL, Greenwich, CT
Head Coach
Teach team members fundamentals of baseball. Evaluate playing skills and offer technical advice. Schedule practices and assign playing positions. Lead fitness program. Supervise staff of three. Act as liaison to parents.

1984 to Present   GREENWICH ATHLETIC ASSOCIATION BASEBALL, Greenwich, CT
Coach
Coach a team of 10-12 year-olds in competitive basketball.

1984   ANDERVILLE DAY CAMP, Riverside, CT
Counselor
Supervised a group of 20 counselors-in-training (ages 14-15). Provided instruction in counseling skills. Led group instructional sessions. Organized recreational activities for the unit, including overnight trips.

REFERENCES   References and academic records are available on request.

```
SALES REPRESENTATIVE
Sample Resume
```

DIANA MAE SWENSON
458 Lakeview Drive, Apt. 330
Nashua, New Hampshire 61689
(603) 691-9544 (home)

EXPERIENCE: **DISTRICT SALES REPRESENTATIVE** 1989 - present
Rydel Research Corporation, Hudson, New Hampshire

Manage all aspects of the New England sales territory, including meeting the territory's $3.9 million quota, managing the company's largest OEM accounts, supervising distributors in the sales territory, and organizing local sales symposiums.

Accomplishments:

● Exceeded quotas by at least 23% in all quarters.

● Ranked number one salesperson in company, 1989.

SALES REPRESENTATIVE 1987 - 1989
Rydel Research Corporation, Teaneck, NJ

Established the company's first New Jersey regional sales office. Established and managed distributors and OEMs in the territory. Managed office operations.

Accomplishments:

● Exceeded the territory's $2.5 million quota.

PUBLIC RELATIONS COORDINATOR 1986 - 1987
PUBLIC RELATIONS INTERN Summer 1985
Norbotics Incorporated, Nashua, NH

Managed all corporate public relations activities. Wrote press releases, backgrounders and specification sheets. Arranged press conferences and press tours. Secured speaking engagements for company employees and customers at industry seminars. Planned annual user group meetings.

Accomplishments:

● Developed and maintained the company's first consultant database.

● Managed all aspects of Norbotics' national and regional tradeshows, including developing show calendar, managing tradeshow budgets, designing exhibits, and overseeing exhibit properties.

● Produced pre-event direct mail promotions for tradeshows that increased booth traffic by 38%.

EDUCATION: Syracuse University, Syracuse, NY December 1985
Summa cum laude   GPA: 3.9/4.0
Class rank: 1 out of 447

Dual degree program:

Bachelor of Science in Advertising
S.I. Newhouse School of Public Communications

Bachelor of Science in Marketing
School of Management

References furnished upon request

MILDRED KOPFKY
9 Birch Hill Circle
Lexington, Kentucky 76173
(678) 782-8153

SUMMARY

Highly skilled administrative secretary with excellent organizational, communications, and clerical skills.

- Type 70+ wpm with excellent accuracy.
- Know numerous word processing systems, including DECMATE I & II, Lanier, Mass 11, WordPerfect.
- Make all arrangements for meetings and conferences. Reserve rooms, order meals, arrange seating, coordinate schedules, get security clearances for guests.
- Write and edit correspondence.
- Train new secretarial staff.

PROFESSIONAL EXPERIENCE

THE DANTRE CORPORATION, Lexington, KY
Senior Secretary   1978 to Present

Provide administrative and secretarial support. Work with confidential material. Offer typing and word processing, prepare funding proposals, monitor expense vouchers, arrange meetings and travel, edit agendas, train new staff.

Accomplishments
- Hold top-secret security clearance.
- Promoted to this position within one year.
- Reorganized office organization systems, greatly increasing efficiency and reducing lost files.
- Appointed computer resource person for department.

TAX ASSESSOR'S OFFICE, Lexington, Kentucky
Secretary   1976 to 1977
Provided customer service. Dealt with irate customers, kept track of accounts, sent out billing notices. Wrote correspondence using DECMATE and WordPerfect. Trained new staff on word processing skills.

EDUCATION

UNIVERSITY OF ALABAMA, Birmingham, Ala.
Major: Education

COURSES in Business Writing & Editing, Management Skills, Administrative Secretary Skills at DANTRE Institute.

ACTIVITIES

COORDINATOR, Rosie's Meal Delivery Program (1989)
Recruited volunteers, solicited food donations, and coordinated food delivery to Rosie's, a shelter for homeless people.

COORDINATOR, Bloodmobile Program (1988 to Present)
Coordinate volunteers and act as Red Cross liaison.

REFERENCES   Available upon request

> **SMALL BUSINESS OWNER**
> Sample Resume

SUSAN F. CLARK
6 Renu Circle
Taos, New Mexico 78280
(309) 722-5311

SUMMARY

Proficient **SMALL BUSINESS OWNER AND MANAGER** with extensive experience in buying, administration, merchandising, and developing excellent customer relations.

* Established 11 years in business.

* Doubled retail sales within several years.

* Developed well-attended Artisan's Workshop Series.

* Successful clothing designer, graphic and fine artist.

PROFESSIONAL EXPERIENCE

SMALL BUSINESS OWNER (1979 to Present)
Splendid Gifts, Taos, New Mexico

Developed this unique gift and crafts store from the ground floor. Buy all merchandise from over 72 vendors, develop displays and promotional campaigns, hire and supervise staff, administer all aspects of the business.

Accomplishments:

● Developed excellent reputation for product mix and service.

● Doubled sales and customer base.

● Expanded physical location two times to accommodate increasing traffic.

● Broadened business climate in area.

● Introduced Artisan Education Workshops at store, receiving note in the Guild of American Craftsmen publication.

● Developed show at the Children's Museum of Boston that received special commendation from the museum.

PRACTICING FINE ARTIST (1970 to Present)

Studied with renowned artists Gracia Dayton and George Gabin. Created over one thousand pieces of fine art with excellence in several mediums. Illustrated publications, cassette covers, product packaging for major accounts including Bay Banks and Beth Israel Hospital (Boston, MA).

Accomplishments:

● Solo show at Gallery Chimaron, Albuquerque, New Mexico.

● Sponsored and developed all aspects of group show, Unitarian Church, Taos, NM.

● Designed and sold over 400 original paintings on clothing.

● Exhibits include Taos Arts, New Mexico Art Association, and several throughout the country.

TEACHER (1979 to Present)

Offer stress reduction and meditation classes throughout the Southwest. Taught classes at the University of Arizona, the University of New Mexico, and Texas State University. Guided over 2,700 students.

SUSAN F. CLARK
Page 2

Accomplishments:

● Featured on WSBH Television and WEGN Radio.

● Profiled in four articles in major newspapers.

● Guest speaker at the Taos Women's Writing Group and the Universalist Church of Taos.

● Coordinated final ceremony, Albuquerque City Hall, for Peace Run 1989.

MANAGER (1975 to 1979)
Altrecht Boutique, Boston, MA

Oversaw merchandising and displays. Purchased merchandise, including travel. Trained employees.
Managed financial records. Offered profit share in company for excellent performance.

EDUCATION

MASSACHUSETTS COLLEGE OF ART, Boston, MA (1975-79)
Major in Illustration
* Special honors in drawing
* Worked way through school

UNIVERSITY OF NOTRE DAME, South Bend, Indiana
Major in Fine Arts
* Selected for year-abroad program.
* Received honors for thesis on Soren Kierkegard.

ADDITIONAL TRAINING includes courses at Montserrat College, the Art Institute of Boston, and
the Southwest Artist Week with Gracia Dayton.

ORGANIZATIONS

* Member, The Guild of American Craftsmen.

* Member, The Taos Chamber of Commerce.

* Member, The Small Business Association of America.

* Member, New Mexico Small Business Association.

ACTIVITIES

Completed six marathons. Acted in New York productions. Singing performances at the Southwest
Cultural Convention and on Channel 56.

References provided upon request.

ANDREA F. BALESTEIN
6 Alteridge Road
Atlanta, Georgia 71986
(609) 692-5121

HIGHLIGHTS

* *Software developer* with broad experience in software and systems design, analysis, and product documentation.

* *Project leader/manager* with experience supervising staff and overseeing all aspects of development from conception to shipping.

* *Seek* staff position with progressive company utilizing my technical expertise and management ability.

TECHNICAL EXPERTISE

HARDWARE: Data General, Digital, Honeywell, Interdata, IBM, RCA, Raytheon, and Burroughs systems.

LANGUAGES: Assembly, C, COBOL, FORTRAN, BASIC, MUMPS, CP/M, DATATRIEVE, RDML, TAPS, and Microprogramming. Familiar with C++.

SYSTEMS SOFTWARE: Assemblers, editors, interpreters, filters, compilers (MUMPS and BASIC), drivers and diagnostics for computers and typesetters. Familiar with X-Windows, UNIX, and desktop publishers including Interleaf.

BUSINESS APPLICATIONS: Accounts payable/receivable, payroll, inventory control, records processing, order and billing, communications, graphics, word processing, medical systems, and database design.

PROFESSIONAL EXPERIENCE

SOFTWARE ENGINEER/CONSULTANT
Adaptive Systems, Inc., Atlanta, Georgia (1978 to Present)
Managed numerous software development projects for a wide range of clients, including (selected list):

DIGITAL EQUIPMENT CORPORATION: Wrote a filter that converted Genegraphics to REGIS code, merging text and graphics library files. Designed and wrote a filter to convert IBM 5520 DCA/RFT files to Interleaf save-ASCII files. Wrote a video production tracking system. Designed programs to convert databases to typeset output. Developed WPS-8 word processor enhancements. Designed disk editors and handlers. *Called back on numerous projects in recognition of outstanding performance.*

EVERETT RESEARCH LABORATORIES, INC.: Designed a post-mission processing system for a real-time airborne sensor, in coordination with a team. Participated in system design, programmed, developed testing and file management systems. *Completed project under-budget, within eight months.*

RAYTHEON: Implemented Fault Analysis module for Direct Radar Access Control (DARC) system. Developed pioneering, exceptionally effective testing procedures.

AVIATION RESPONSE, INC. (A.R.I.), Philadelphia, PA: Implemented CLAMP (Closed Loop Aeronautical Management Program), a multitasking message-switching system. Installed new operating systems, introduced new languages and backup procedures. Acted as troubleshooter for all system and software problems.

ANDREA F. BALESTEIN
Page 2

MANAGER OF ENGINEERING SOFTWARE
Design Systems Inc., Macon, Georgia (1976-78)

Supervised six programmers, including hiring, training, and performance evaluations. Scheduled projects. Oversaw development of all software products, including editors, typesetters, and customized programs. Developed new bug-reporting systems that facilitated rapid problem solving. Implemented highly effective testing procedures.

Accomplishments:

• Significantly improved documentation for both internal and external customers.

• Supervised release of over 100 products in two years.

• Updated company's software products to make them completely modular.

SENIOR PROGRAMMER ANALYST
Photex Inc., Wilmington, Delaware (1972-76)

Provided project leadership in designing and implementing a phototypesetting system with capability for later conversion to ROM. Acted as in-house NOVA specialist, with overall responsibility for system generation, file maintenance procedures, and RDOS operation and programming. Developed Electronic Mask Making Apparatus (EMMA) — a photo plotter. Developed software interface for EMMA, assembler for Photon controller, and database for computerized ordering system. Provided pre- and post-sales support, system installation, and customer training.

EDUCATION

BOSTON UNIVERSITY, Boston, MA
Bachelor of Science in Engineering Management
Minor in Mechanical Engineering

ADDITIONAL TRAINING includes Data General Sales Training (1979), a full-time three-month program.

COMMUNITY LEADERSHIP

Elected to Atlanta School Committee for 12 consecutive years (1973-85). Served on numerous subcommittees, including the Budget Subcommittee and the Computer Needs Subcommittee. Served as School Committee Vice-Chairman, 1975.

Appointed by Mayor to Atlanta Cable Subcommittee and Atlanta Computer Advisory Committee, (1987-Present)

Coach, Atlanta Girls Youth Soccer (1977-88). Won first or second place within league every year.

References provided upon request.

STUDENT
Sample Resume

WILLIAM CAMERON

67 Pickering Road
Augusta, Maine 30198
501-254-2745 (home)
603-864-5581 (school)

HIGHLIGHTS	* Dean's List graduate (May 1991) from the University of New Hampshire with concentrations in Communications and Business.
	* Exceptional track record in student leadership.
	* Work experience managing a fast-paced retail operation and supervising staff, with record of superior performance.
EDUCATION	**UNIVERSITY OF NEW HAMPSHIRE,** Durham, New Hampshire **Bachelor of Arts,** 1991 *Major in Communications with a concentration in Business* Courses include Financial Accounting, Economics, Advertising and Promotion
Honors	* Dean's List multiple semesters. * Work submitted for publication in *COMM-entary* magazine. * National Honor Society, 1984-87. * Carl Fisher Memorial Award in Wrestling, 1987.
Leadership	* Elected Treasurer, Pi Kappa Alpha (1990-91). Manage $35,000 semi-annual budget. * Elected Rush Chairman, Pi Kappa Alpha (1988 - Present). * Elected Intrafraternity Council Rep to Administration, 1990. * Elected Alumni Representative, 1990. * Appointed Captain of Intramural Sports Team.
BACKGROUND	● Supervised up to 20 employees, recruited staff, provided training, oversaw scheduling. ● Managed all operations for several food service establishments seating up to 60 people. Oversaw product ordering and took inventory. Dealt with vendors. Managed kitchen operations. ● Assumed ultimate responsibility for insuring customer satisfaction and handling customer complaints. ● Received superior evaluations in all positions. Promoted three times in three years. Earned bonuses for exceptional performance. ● Know Macintosh computer software and operation. ● Never missed a day of work in any position.
WORK HISTORY	**Kitchen Manager,** *Market Street Pizza,* Mashpee, MA (Summer 1990) **Banquet Manager,** *Alan Party Tent,* Mashpee, MA (Summer 1989) **Manager,** *Pizza Poppy,* New Seabury, MA (Promoted three times from position of Counter Help, Summers 1984-88)
ACTIVITIES	Enjoy ocean sports, wrestling, golf. CPR Certified.

STEPHEN JUDGE
11 Power Lane
Westfield, MA 11623
(413) 557-3468

SUMMARY OF QUALIFICATIONS

Expertise as a **Systems Manager** and **Software Developer**, with special knowledge of Digital VAX-cluster systems. Additional experience as a Personal Computer Instructor.

TECHNICAL EXPERTISE

Languages: FORTRAN, COBOL, DCL, C, GKS, Data Manipulation Language, Query Language Processing, Dbase III +, Executive Control Language.

Operating Systems: DOS, VMS, UNIX, UNISYS

Software: Experience developing a wide array of software programs including graphics, statistical, and accounting packages.

PROFESSIONAL EXPERIENCE

SYSTEMS MANAGEMENT/SOFTWARE DEVELOPMENT (1989 to Present)
MIT Geophysics Lab, **Atmospheric Science Division**, Westfield, MA

Develop software to maximize the accuracy of short-range weather forecasting systems using satellite and radar imagery. Utilize FORTRAN, C, DCL, and graphical interface utilities. Also manage a Local Area Vax Cluster (LAVC) consisting of 17 nodes and supporting 35 users. Maintain user accounts, monitor system performance and hardware, perform system backups, install upgrades, troubleshoot system problems and provide technical support to users.

Accomplishments:

- Appointed to assume the additional responsibilities of System Manager in 1990.
- Designed, wrote, debugged, documented, and executed a comprehensive system — including image processing, statistical database, spreadsheet, and evaluation software components — to statistically evaluate the accuracy of new forecasting techniques.
- Developed a numerical weather model animation capability that was named a *Significant Event* in nationally distributed Air Force Newsletter, and that led to savings of $15K to $20K in contract costs.

BASE LEVEL OPERATIONS PROGRAMMER (1987 to 1989)
United States Air Force, Wells Air Force Base, Columbus, Ohio
Overseas Communications Division

Redesigned Pacific National Payroll system to create a relational database, in coordination with a team. Developed personal computer program management system using Dbase III + software. Performed program maintenance and troubleshooting on three payroll and accounting systems (based in the Philippines). Implemented system improvements, corresponding with users by telephone or by travel to the site.

Accomplishments:

- Received Air Force Commendation Medal, August 1989.
- Developed system improvements that saved over 1000 hours of processing time.
- Developed software capability for payroll database that immediately incorporated newly entered information.

PERSONAL COMPUTER INSTRUCTOR (1988 to 1989)
United States Air Force, Wells Air Force Base, Columbus, Ohio
A part-time, contract position.

Taught classes of up to 15 students in Enable Software, Microsoft Disk Operating System, DBase III +
programming, and BASIC programming. Designed curriculum, developed course materials, and
offered follow-up support to students. Consistently received excellent evaluations from students,
most of whom enrolled in follow-up classes.

TROBOPROP PROPULSION MECHANIC (1984 to 1987)
United States Air Force, Bay City, Michigan

Performed repair and maintenance on various aircraft. Supervised five crew members and provided
in-depth on-the-job training. *Received Air Force Achievement Medal for Meritorious
Service, 1987.*

BOOKKEEPER (1983)
Rand Corporation, Marketing Division, Quincy, MA

EDUCATION

BACHELOR OF SCIENCE IN COMPUTER APPLICATIONS, 1988
University of Ohio. Additional coursework in business, mathematics. *Maintained 3.34 average.*

ADVANCED COURSES at Digital Equipment Corporation (Bedford, MA), The Learning Tree
(Virginia), American Institute (New York), and the USAF. Courses include over 400 hours of
training in data communications, systems management, and programming subjects (see attached list).

ADDITIONAL HONORS

- Received **highest rating** in all Performance Reports, 1985 to 1990.

- Received **Good Conduct Medal**, USAF, 1990, 1987.

- Awarded **Outstanding Unit Award**, USAF, 1986.

- Promoted to ES Staff Sergeant within five years, one year less than average.

REFERENCES

Provided upon request.

TEACHER (ECE)
Sample Resume

CHRISTINE KOSLOW
83 Bachelor Drive
Plainview, NY 59032
(516) 832-5557

PROFESSIONAL EXPERIENCE

TUTOR
Professional Teachers, Inc., East Norwich, NY   1987 to Present
Teach reading and math skills to children, grades K-6, in their homes. Also teach ESL to
Asian-American children.

DIRECTOR
Hauppage Day School, Hauppage, NY   1976 to 1987
Founded and directed this school for children ages K-3. Obtained registration from State Education
Department. Recruited and supervised interns and teachers. Personally taught a heterogeneous K-3
class.

Accomplishments
- Effected growth in enrollment from six children to 55.
- Established specialty programs in French, science, and music.
- Initiated and directed use of open classrooms, Frostic perceptual development materials,
  Cuisenaire and Nuffield math materials, and Montessori sensorial materials.

HEAD TEACHER
Willow Cooperative Day School, Huntington, NY   1971 to 1976
Taught classes of three and four year olds. Supervised parents in the classroom. Organized periodic
conferences with parents and the school psychologist. Selected appropriate teaching materials for the
school via catalogs, trades shows, and suppliers.

Accomplishments
- Introduced perceptual development materials to the school.
- Initiated use of an indoor gym to create an easy flow between classrooms.

EDUCATION

SUNY, College at Old Westbury, Old Westbury, NY
B.S. in Early Childhood Education, 1976
GPA: 4.0   Graduated Summa Cum Laude.

- Received APEX Certification, Pre-K through 6.

ADDITIONAL TRAINING includes numerous in-service courses, annual workshops, and conferences
sponsored by the Early Education Council and BOCES R&D Division.

REFERENCES

Available upon request

MALCOLM KOEDYKER
PSC #7, Box 591
Tyler Air Force Base
Tyler, Texas
(512) 634-6731

SUMMARY OF QUALIFICATIONS

Television Director/Master Control Operator/Video Tape Editor with twenty years of experience in all phases of television and radio production.

AREAS OF EXPERTISE

Technical/Creative
- Overseeing all aspects of production, including shooting, directing, staging, set design, audio, and editing.
- Writing scripts for television and radio, including ads, informational shows, theme programs, and news shows.
- Developing, selecting, and monitoring programming for a variety of audiences.

Broadcast Management
- Maintaining and cataloging audiovisual libraries.
- Developing operational logs and procedures.
- Ordering, evaluating, and monitoring equipment and supplies.
- Training and supervising personnel.

Production Equipment
- Utilize numerous editors, including SONY, BVU 5600 up to BVU 950s, including 1" Ampex.
- Have worked with ENG, RCA, Panasonic, and JVC cameras.
- Familiar with Chryon VP2 Character Generator and Quanta.
- Know numerous audio boards, including Paintbox, Grass Valley Switchers, etc.

PROFESSIONAL EXPERIENCE

1969 to Present

ARMED FORCES RADIO AND TELEVISION SERVICES, United States Air Force
Held a variety of positions, including:

Channel C-12, Tyler Air Force Base (1989-Present)
Chief of Television Operations
Oversee closed-circuit cable station for internal communications. Develop programming, including writing scripts for news and feature shows. Produce, direct, and tape live shows and do ENG work. Supervise staff. Upgrade equipment. Advise management on status of operations.

Armed Forces Network (AFN), Saudi Arabia (1987-88)
Master Control Operator, Asst. Program Director, NCOIC
Selected and scheduled programming for TV station broadcasting to 60,000 military viewers and to shadow audience of all Saudi citizens. Worked with NBC to provide coverage of the Olympics, marking the first time in history a military broadcast company worked with a commercial company. Catalogued over 10,000 tapes and maintained audiovisual library. Selected and maintained production materials including 3/4" video tapes, 16mm films, and 1" tapes. Acted as Master Control Operator. Supervised staff.

Navy Broadcasting Service, Honolulu, Hawaii (1986-87)
NCOIC TV Programming/Staff Announcer/Master Control Operator
Selected and scheduled programming for two cable channels using satellite and internal programming. Compiled program guides. Produced local news show, call-in show, and "People in the News" show. Wrote scripts. Managed film library. Supervised staff. Taped live show using 3/4" tape. Produced radio spots. Acted as announcer for "Midnight Crossing" radio show. Filled all production roles in times of personnel shortages (lighting, props, audio, technical directing, etc.).

Non-Commissioned Officer in Charge of Media Relations
Assistant Deputy of Public Affairs
Developed and produced "Ellsworth Update," a weekly news program to inform the public of events at the Base. Arranged national media and local media coverage for critical events at the Base. Provided escort and arranged media coverage for visiting British Strategic Air Team.

Armed Forces Network (AFKN), Berlin, Germany
Program Director/Working News/Electronic News
Covered over 45 ENG events, resulting in letters of appreciation from Boy Scouts of Germany, German Mountain Club, and a plaque from Leipzig University. Oversaw promotion, managed library, kept logs, produced and edited video programs, covered satellite events, wrote scripts.

PREVIOUS POSITIONS WITH THE
ARMED FORCES RADIO AND TELEVISION SERVICES

- Started as a Production Assistant in 1969.
- Station Program Director, Ubon, Thailand.
- Non-Commissioned Officer in Charge of Productions, Torrejon, Spain.
- Radio and TV Broadcast Specialist, Seoul, Korea.

HONORS AND AWARDS

- Armed Achievement Medal for coverage of Team Spirit '82.
- Air Force Commendation Medal for development of original program schedule using taped and live events.
- Air Force Commendation Medal for shut-down of AFTN in Ubon, Thailand.
- Outstanding Television Audio Engineer Award, Graham Junior College, for coverage of 1966 political campaign.

EDUCATION

1979 to 82   Troy State University, Troy, Alabama
              Major: Resource Management

1966-68   Graham Junior College, Boston, MA
              Major: Television Production

1977   Air Force Supervisor's Correspondence Course

REFERENCES   Available upon request

```
┌─────────────────────┐
│ VIDEOGRAPHER        │
│ Sample Resume       │
└─────────────────────┘
```

ZHONGCHI YAN
47 Fairmont Lane
Danbury, Connecticut 52735
(203) 244-8907

SUMMARY

Award winning **VIDEOGRAPHER/PRODUCER/EDITOR** with outstanding record of accomplishment in educational documentary. Additional track record creating highly successful promotional and instructional media for colleges and schools.

PROFESSIONAL EXPERIENCE

YAN & ASSOCIATES PRODUCTIONS, New Haven, CT (1983 to Present)
Formerly Yan & Davis Productions, Yan-Browne Productions
Producer/Videographer/Editor

Produce, shoot, and edit educational documentaries, professional development videos for educators, and unique promotional videos for independent schools, colleges, and universities. Coordinate all aspects of production, from conception to final edit. Oversee administration of the company. Built business from ground floor to $220,000 annual revenues. Major projects include:

Educational Documentary

● *The Coalition of Essential Schools,* Yale University, 1989-1990

> Produced, shot, and edited a series of documentaries presenting a new model for secondary education, distributed to politicians, administrators, and teachers nationwide. Series includes five tapes portraying a case study of a High School in Harlem and a provocative 1/2 hour tape entitled "Student as Worker." Series was so powerful and successful that the Coalition received numerous requests to purchase even the incomplete rough edit.

● *Performance Based Assessment,* 1990

> Produced, shot, and edited a series of five tapes exploring alternate methods for evaluating academic performance (performance-based assessment), in conjunction with Dr. Grant Wiggins. Shot classrooms throughout the nation, performing in-depth research on the politics, problems, and personnel in each school.

● *Eight Secrets of Great Teaching*

> Under a grant from the Geraldine R. Dodge Foundation, produced, shot, and edited this video now used as a key component of the teaching curriculum at such schools as New York University and Marshall University. Approved for airing on the Learning Channel. Received outstanding reviews.

Promotional Videos, 1983-Present

> Produced, shot, and edited numerous promotional videos for such institutions as Phillips Andover Academy, Wheelock College, and the Ethel Walker School. Use intimate style of shooting and unique approach, relying on interviews with students and teachers at the school rather than on traditional sales methods. Highly successful results generated numerous awards and letters of commendation.

ACHIEVEMENTS:

● Awarded Gold Medal, Council for the Advance and Support of Education (CASE), Washington, D.C., for promotional video, 1989.

● Awarded CASE Gold, Silver, and Bronze Medals for promotional videos, 1988. Awarded Silver and Bronze Medals in 1987.

ZHONGCHI YAN
Page 2

- Won Admissions Marketing Report Merit Award for Roger Williams College promotional video, 1988.
- Featured panelist on video production, NAIS Conference, 1986, 1988-89.
- Invited workshop leader, CASE Conference on Video, 1991. Presented, *Using In-House Talent to Provide Narrative Structure in Video Tapes*.
- Received letters of commendation from Brown University and numerous other clients for documentary work and promotional videos.
- Professional development videos selected for presentation at several international teleconferences, including North Central Regional Educational Laboratory and the State of New Mexico.
- Filmed more than 250 classrooms nationwide; conducted 400+ interviews.
- Completed all jobs on time and within budget.

ALAN LEIWORTH PRODUCTIONS, New Haven, CT (1978-82)
Product Developer

Originated concept for several highly successful instructional software packages still marketed through McGraw Hill. Performed research; wrote a *Teacher Guide* and *Student Guide* for each package. Co-designed product. Programs included:

- Community Search. This year-long simulation game teaches students about cultural assimilation and adaptation.
- Archaeology Search. This two-month simulation teaches students about the Archaeologist's role.

PREVIOUS POSITIONS include 12 years of teaching experience for students in grades 6 through 9, at private schools in Cambridge (Shady Hill School, Montessori School) and Winchester (Lincoln School), Massachusetts. Acted as head teacher in all positions. Created innovative math, science, and social studies curriculum. Trained graduate school apprentice teachers.

EDUCATION

LESLEY COLLEGE, Cambridge, Massachusetts
Master of Education, 1974 4.0 average

UNIVERSITY OF MASSACHUSETTS/AMHERST
Bachelor of Business Administration and Finance, 1971

* *Had two weekly radio shows on WMUA, Amherst, 1970-71.*

INTERESTS

Photography: Photographs published by Allyn & Bacon, 1974, in French Textbook.

Other interests include running, cabinetmaking, building musical instruments, bicycling.

References provided upon request.

```
WAREHOUSE MANAGER
Sample Resume
```

ANTHONY TRICOLI
9-A Clarendon Gardens
Union, NJ
(201) 633-6495

HIGHLIGHTS

● Extensive experience supervising staffs of up to 15 people, including hiring, firing, training, and implementing disciplinary action when necessary.

● Proven track record motivating people to succeed and garnering outside financial support.

● Experience assuming overall managerial experience, including designing administrative procedures, evaluating programs and staff, writing reports.

● Assuming final responsibility for handling and storage of vast inventories of fragile merchandise, valued up to $2,000,000.

PROFESSIONAL EXPERIENCE

WAREHOUSE MANAGER
Seidel Inc., Elizabeth, NJ (1981 to Present)
Promoted from position as Inside Sales Representative in 1983.

● Supervise staff of 15 shippers, receivers, and custodial personnel. Provide training, issue verbal and written evaluations, institute disciplinary procedures, oversee hiring and firing.

● Oversee storage and maintenance of approximately $2,000,000 in inventory; also oversee equipment; order supplies as needed.

● Insure timely and efficient shipping and receipt of all merchandise.

● As Inside Sales Representative, provided customer service to retail customers, processed orders, investigated and resolved customer problems.

Accomplishments:

   ● Designed overall warehouse organization and layout.

   ● Instituted quality control procedures resulting in considerable savings to company.

   ● Member of Sales Group that received numerous plaques for exceeding sales quotas (1981-83).

SUPERVISOR
Brini Brothers International, Newark, NJ (1971 to 1981)
Promoted from position as a production worker (1971-73)

Oversaw staff of six production personnel for this plumbing supplies manufacturer. Set employee schedules, tracked hours, evaluated employee performance, recommended raises. Taught safety and maintenance procedures to staff. Oversaw maintenance of shop, including insuring compliance with OSHA safety standards. Insured upkeep and proper application of all production equipment. Repaired faulty equipment when necessary.

EDUCATION

COLUMBIA UNIVERSITY, New York, NY
Courses in Math, Economics and English
Received 3.5 and above in major subjects.

AMSTED INSTITUTE, Newark, NJ
Program in Electrical Circuitry

ANTHONY TRICOLI
Page 2

COMMUNITY ACTIVITIES

COACH, National Softball Team (1974 to Present)
Developed local team to national status. Garnered support of major sponsors, including MVP Sports, raising up to $20,000. Managed budget. Brought team to 591 victories, with only 230 losses. Scheduled games, made travel arrangements, coached individual team members, played actively on team as pitcher.

COACH, Union Little League (1985 - Present)
Offered support and coaching to 15 youths aged 9 to 12.

REFERENCES

Provided upon request.

| WASTE MANAGEMENT PROFESSIONAL |
| Sample Resume |

ROBERT OTTLINGER
470 Periton Parkway
Miami, Florida 05987
(608) 573-7745

SUMMARY

Highly experienced manager in the solid waste management field, with proven ability to run a profitable business and strong sales/sales management skills.

HIGHLIGHTS

- Consistently increased sales and profits in all positions.
- Thorough knowledge of recycling industry.
- Expertise in the selection and application of hydraulic compaction equipment.
- Expertise recruiting and supervising staffs of considerable size.

PROFESSIONAL EXPERIENCE

1987 to Present

DISPOSAL, INC., Miami, Florida
Director of Operations/General Manager
Oversee day-to-day operations of a highly profitable six-million dollar independent refuse hauling company engaged in industrial, commercial, and residential refuse removal. Manage multiple divisions; insure increasing productivity; handle contract negotiation and analysis, acquisition of subsidiary companies, route analysis; oversee purchase of equipment; recruit staff.

1986 to 1987

GERWIN INDUSTRIES, Cincinnati, Ohio
Northeast Regional Sales Manager
Increased sales from $100,000 to $1,000,000 and set up a distributor network in New England territory. Company emphasizes transfer stations, live floor trailers, and compactors.

1980 to 1985

RADVIL, INC., Knoxville, TN
Special Accounts Manager
Developed and serviced national accounts, including Waste Management, Inc., BFI, SCA, City of Atlanta and New York City. Formulated, managed, and monitored strong distributor networks as sales strategy. Promoted from:

Northeast District Sales Manager
Evaluated efficiency of distributors from Canada to Virginia and reorganized territories, resulting in a significant increase in volume. Formulated marketing plans, coordinated sales force, added new distributors, established previously closed national accounts.

1975 to 1980

KNOX SERVICES, Boston, MA
Sales/Service Manager
Organized recycling program for industrial and municipal customers. Identified new markets, solicited customers, consulted with architects on design of transfer stations. Oversaw Compaction Sales and Service Departments. Coordinated rebuilding and installation of compactors.

EDUCATION

UNIVERSITY OF OHIO, Columbus, Ohio
Bachelor of Science in Education

REFERENCES

Available upon request

Willing to Travel/Relocate

SUZANNE RHETT-WINGER
79 East 49th Street, Apartment 23A
New York, NY 10023
(212) 479-7023

PROFESSIONAL EXPERTISE

Writing

- Considerable experience writing reports, articles, proposals, and newsletters for major corporations.
- Numerous publications in national magazines including *The Atlantic Monthly, Redbook,* and *The New York Times* (see attached publications list).
- Author of three non-fiction books (see attached publications list).
- Received award from *The Washington Post* for writing "One of the Three Best Articles of 1990." Also received the *Writer's Digest Award* for best non-fiction acticle, 1989.
- Extensive background writing technical and scientific materials.
- Experience producing charts, graphics, and layout designs.

Administration

- Considerable experience overseeing all administrative functions for writing organizations including developing record-keeping systems, assigning responsibilities, and managing work flow.
- Experience hiring, training, and supervising freelancers and permanent staff.
- Proven ability to design and implement successful promotional campaigns, including producing materials, building media relations, and speaking in public.

Teaching

- Teach writing seminars and classes at major universities throughout the Northeast.
- Design curriculum and write training manuals, course materials, and learning programs for corporate and academic clients.

WORK HISTORY

WORDS FIRST, New York, NY (1984 to Present)   **Managing Editor/Writer**
Offer writing, editing, training, and research services. Oversee administration, hire subcontractors, spearhead promotional efforts. Recent clients include (partial list; see attached Client List for complete roster):

  DIGITAL EQUIPMENT CORPORATION: Wrote training materials and product guides.

  TELDYNE: Wrote scientific manuscripts, proposals, and marketing materials; edited company newsletter; created graphics.

  THE WALL STREET JOURNAL: Contributing writer.

  THE NEW YORK TIMES: Contributing writer.

  MACY'S: Wrote promotional materials and stockholder reports.

  LOTUS DEVELOPMENT CORPORATION: Wrote reference manual and specification guidelines for a new OS/2 graphics program.

  TRAINING RESOURCES (Philadelphia): Wrote video scripts and training materials.

  NEW YORK TELEPHONE COMPANY: Wrote training manuals for accounting managers.

  COLUMBIA UNIVERSITY: Instruct two writing courses.

SUZANNE RHETT-WINGER
Page 2

HOFSTRA UNIVERSITY (1984-88)
Publications Coordinator, Dean's Office
Oversaw publication of all school catalogs, newspapers, and promotional materials. Hired and supervised a staff of 13. Wrote feature articles for the school paper, produced catalog copy. Hired freelancers and outside contractors. Oversaw the entire production process.

● *Introduced successful new staff newspaper.*

● *Won award from National Council of University Publications for redesign of the school catalog.*

ALDUS SOFTWARE (1983-84)
Chief Technical Writer
Served as chief technical writer for the company. Acted as Product Manager for *Pagemaker* software. Analyzed software products and recommended improvements. Wrote manuals for 10 software products. Wrote help screens, trained users, tested products.

● *Won STC Annual Award for Pagemaker documentation.*

COLUMBIA STAFF UNION (1984 to Present)
Instructor in Meditation
Teach meditation classes to students, staff, and faculty members.

SYMPHONY, INC., Philadelphia, PA (1981-84)
Chief Writer/Editor
Ghostwriter for *Symphony*, a self-help guide. Wrote and edited learning programs and promotional materials. Performed research. Coordinated acquisition of materials. Hired and supervised staff.

THE YOUTH EMPLOYMENT PROGRAM, Pittsburgh, PA (1975-79)
Director
Supervised staff of 21. Developed innovative career training program. Oversaw job development and program administration.

EDUCATION

UNIVERSITY OF PENNSYLVANIA, Philadelphia, PA (1979-80)
M.A. in English
Received Florence Dowd Fellowship for excellence in creative writing.

STATE UNIVERSITY OF NEW YORK AT STONY BROOK
B.S., Human Development, Summa Cum Laude (1975)
GPA: 3.92

ADDITIONAL COURSES in writing and photography at Sarah Lawrence, Columbia, and the Metropolitan Museum School, 1982-88.

ACTIVITIES

Member of PEN Women, the Freelance Editorial Association, and The National Writers Union.

Completed seven marathons. Enjoy photography, writing humor, playing cello.

Served as Northeast Coordinator for Peace Run '89, an event involving thousands of participants.

References available upon request.

APPENDIX 3

HELPFUL RESOURCES

Thousands of books, journals, agencies, and other resources are available to help you in your job search. Some of the most useful are listed below:

HELPFUL BOOKS

All-Around Great Resource

What Color Is Your Parachute? by Richard Bolles (Ten Speed Press). Many people consider this book the job-hunter's bible. It provides lots of wise advice about how to identify your strengths, choose the right job, and market yourself successfully. And, it includes a comprehensive resource directory that lists career counselors by state, plus helpful books, materials, and organizations. *Parachute* gets updated annually.

For Information about How to Find a Job

Careering and Re-Careering for the 1990s, by Ronald L. Krannich (Impact Publications, 1989).

The Complete Job Search Handbook: All the Skills You Need to Get Any Job and Have a Good Time Doing It, by Howard Figler, Ph.D. (Henry Holt, 1988).

Go Hire Yourself an Employer, by Richard K. Irish (Anchor Press/Doubleday, 1987).

Guerilla Tactics in the Job Market: A Practical Manual, by Tom Jackson (Bantam Books, 1980).

How to Get a Better Job Quicker, by Richard A. Payne (Taplinger Publishing Company, 1987).

How to Sell Yourself in an Interview, by Arthur R. Pell, Ph.D. (Monarch, 1982).

The New York Times Career Planner, by Elizabeth M. Fowler (Times Books, 1987).

The Robert Half Way to Get Hired in Today's Job Market, by Robert Half (Rawson Wade Publishers).

For Information about Where to Find Jobs

The Complete Guide to International Jobs and Careers, by Krannich and Krannich (Impact Publications, 1990).

Good Works: A Guide to Careers in Social Change, by Joan Anzalone (Dembner Books, New York, 1985).

How to Be Happily Employed in Boston, How to Be Happily Employed in Dallas-Fort Worth, How to Be Happily Employed in San Francisco, How to Be Happily Employed in Washington, D.C., all edited by Janice Benjamin and Barbara Block (Random House, 1990).

1991 Internships (updated annually), by Brian Rushig (Peterson's Guides).

Jobs '91, by Kathryn and Ross Petras (Prentice Hall, 1991).

The National Job Bank, edited by Carter Smith (Bob Adams, updated annually). Lists summary of company, types of jobs typically available, contact person, and phone number for companies in every state.

The 100 Best Companies to Work for in America, by Robert Levering, Milton Moskowitz, and Michael Katz (Addison-Wesley Publishing Company, 1984).

Regional Job Banks (*The Atlanta Job Bank, The Boston Job Bank, The Chicago Job Bank*, etc.) All published by Bob Adams and updated annually. Also available for: Dallas, Denver, Detroit, Florida, Houston, Los Angeles, Minneapolis, New York, Ohio, Philadelphia, Phoenix, San Francisco, Seattle, St. Louis, and Washington, D.C.

Summer Employment Directory of the United States, edited by Pat Beusterien (Writer's Digest Books, updated annually).

For Help in Choosing a Career

The American Almanac of Jobs and Salaries, by John W. Wright and Edward Dwyer (Avon Books, 1990).

The Career Information Center (Glencoe Publishing Company, 1990). This is a 13-part encyclopedia providing detailed information about numerous careers. Includes salary information, employment outlook, and training needed.

What to Do with the Rest of Your Life, by the Catalyst Staff (Simon & Schuster, 1980).

Where Do I Go from Here with My Life?, by John C. Crystal and Richard Bolles (Ten Speed Press).

For Help in Changing Careers

Robert Gerberg's Job Changing System, by Robert Gerberg (Andrews, McMell, and Parker, 1984).

For Minority Job-Seekers

It's Never Too Late to Start Over, by Jo Danna, Ph.D. (Palomino Press, 1984).

Job Hunting for the Disabled, by Edith Marks and Adele Lewis (Barrons Educational Series, Inc., 1983).

Reach Your Goals in Spite of the Old-Boy Network: A Guide for African-American Employees, by Mike Duncan (M. E. Duncan & Company, 1990).

WEEKLY NEWSPAPERS FOR JOB HUNTERS

The National Employment Review (Recourse Communications, Warwick, Rhode Island: 1-800-638-0014). Contains articles about job hunting, and classified ads for jobs nationwide. Also lists upcoming job fairs.

The National Business Employment Weekly (Dow Jones & Company, Princeton, New Jersey). Also contains articles about job hunting, and classified ads for jobs nationwide.

FOR HELP FINDING AN EMPLOYMENT COUNSELOR

The Job Bank Guide to Employment Services (Bob Adams) covers 50 states. Costs $129. Try to get it from your library.

The American Association of Counseling and Development (AACD) prints a list of career counselors accredited by them. Call the AACD at 703-823-9800.

Many colleges have low-cost career counseling services available to the public. Check your local schools.

NATIONAL AGENCIES THAT HELP JOB SEEKERS

Federal Job Information Centers. Also known as the "Office of Employment Security." Offers databank of available jobs. Some offices also offer free job search guidance and vocational counseling. Every major city has a Federal Job Information Center. Look in your telephone directory under "Federal Government" to find your local center.

Jewish Vocational Services. A nationwide network that offers career counseling services to the public at low rates. To find the nearest office, call 1-800-735-7934.

Operation ABLE. A network of independent self-help job search groups for older workers. Look in your telephone directory for a local listing, or call the AARP at 1-800-424-2277 for help.

The Association of Part-Time Professionals. An organization that helps job seekers wanting alternative working arrangements. Call the Alexandria, Virginia office at 703-734-7975 for help.

Throughout the country, hundreds of organizations exist that offer group support to unemployed people. Also, numerous organizations offer help to job seekers in specific fields. For lists of these organizations, check *What Color Is Your Parachute?* If you don't find what you want, ask your librarian for help. You can also call a local career counseling center for information about organizations in your locale.